ECONOMIC AND SOCIAL COMMISSION
FOR WESTERN ASIA (ESCWA)

اللجنة الاقتصادية والاجتماعية
لغربى آسيا (الإسكوا)

نشرة السكان والإحصاءات الحيوية في منطقة الإسكوا

BULLETIN ON POPULATION AND VITAL STATISTICS IN THE ESCWA REGION

العدد الحادي عشر
Eleventh Issue

الأمم المتحدة
نيويورك، ٢٠٠٩

UNITED NATIONS
New York, 2009

UNITED NATIONS PUBLICATION
E/ESCWA/SD/2009/4
ISBN. 978-92-1-128326-6
ISSN. 1020-7368
Sales No. B.09.II.L.3
09-0179

Contents / المحتويات

iii

iv

رموز
Symbols

بيانات غير متوفرة ....
ضئيل أو صفر .... -

Data not available ....
Negligible or zero .... -

vii

INTRODUCTION

The Economic and Social Commission for Western Asia (ESCWA) presents the eleventh issue of the Bulletin on Population and Vital Statistics in the ESCWA Region. The Bulletin provides detailed information on the population of the ESCWA region and its vital events: births, deaths, marriages and divorces. It presents this information in three parts: population; fertility and mortality; and marriage and divorce.

In this issue, the Bulletin presents the main indicators for each vital event. These indicators have been computed using national data, weighted by population estimates from the 2006 Revision of the World Population Prospects, prepared by the United Nations Department of Economic and Social Affairs. Annual data series from 2000 to the latest available year are presented. To facilitate monitoring, data by five-year interval from 1990 to 2000 have also been included. The monitoring of vital events requires comparable data over a period of time. ESCWA has compiled data from national statistical yearbooks and vital statistics publications, where available, and from responses by member countries to ESCWA questionnaires. These questionnaires are used to compile additional information from national statistical offices that reflect regional specificities. In 2008, the Statistics Division at ESCWA collaborated with the United Nations Statistics Division in New York in sending questionnaires to member countries. Duplication of effort was thus eliminated and the burden on national statistical offices consequently lessened.

Following revision of the production process in 2007-2008, ESCWA has introduced major changes to produce a completely revised Bulletin, in which both quality and relevance of disseminated data are enhanced. The objective of these changes is to provide a more effective tool for monitoring comparable data and indicators while maintaining ownership by and credit to national sources.

مقدمة

تقدم اللجنة الاقتصادية والاجتماعية لغربي آسيا (الإسكوا) العدد الحادي عشر من نشرة السكان والإحصاءات الحيوية في منطقة الإسكوا، وهو يتضمن معلومات مفصلة عن السكان والوفيات والولادات والوقائع الحيوية، أي الولادات والوفيات والزواج والطلاق. وتعرض هذه المعلومات في ثلاثة فصول: السكان؛ والخصوبة والوفيات؛ والزواج والطلاق.

ويحتوي هذا العدد من النشرة على المؤشرات الرئيسية لكل حدث حيوي، والتي تم احتسابها باستخدام البيانات الوطنية وترجيحها بتقديرات السكان الوطنية والمنشورات في "التوقعات السكانية في العالم: تنقيح عام ٢٠٠٦" التي أعدتها إدارة الشؤون الاقتصادية والاجتماعية في الأمم المتحدة. وترد في هذا العدد سلاسل زمنية بدءاً من عام ٢٠٠٠ حتى آخر سنة متوفرة. وتسهيلاً لعملية رصد المؤشرات وقائع الحيوية التي تتطلب بيانات قابلة للمقارنة تشمل فترة زمنية معينة، أدرجت البيانات وفق فترات من خمس سنوات من عام ١٩٩٠ إلى عام ٢٠٠٠. وجمعت الإسكوا البيانات من النشرات والإحصاءات الوطنية، والمنشورات حول الإحصاءات الحيوية حيثما توفرت، ومن ردود البلدان الأعضاء على الاستبيانات التي أجرتها الإسكوا، وتُوظف هذه الاستبيانات إلى جمع معلومات إضافية تعكس ميزات المنطقة من الأجهزة المركزية للإحصاء. وقد تعاونت إدارة الإحصاء في الإسكوا مع شعبة الإحصاءات التابعة للأمم المتحدة في عام ٢٠٠٨ لإرسال استبيانات إلى البلدان الأعضاء، مقابلة بذلك الجهود المركزية للإحصاء. وبذلك خففت من العبء الملقى على عاتق الأجهزة المركزية للإحصاء.

وفي أعقاب المراجعة التي أجرتها الإسكوا لعملية إصدار النشرة في الفترة ٢٠٠٧-٢٠٠٨، أدخلت تعديلات أساسية على عملية إصدار النشرة، حيث جرى تحسين نوعية البيانات المنشورة وأهميتها. وكان الهدف من هذه التغييرات إنتاج أداة أكثر فعالية في رصد البيانات والمؤشرات القابلة للمقارنة والمحافظة على حقوق الملكية للأجهزة المركزية للإحصاء والاعتراف بدورها.

viii

This issue introduces an inventory of data availability, a comparative inventory of the region that indicates the level of statistical capacity in individual member countries. Assessment of it reveals the extent of data gaps and the improvements that are necessary at the national level. A wider range of indicators is provided than in earlier editions, and the use of charts and analytical text facilitates the interpretation of indicator values and trends, thus better meeting the needs of stakeholders. Furthermore, where available and applicable, it includes spatial distribution and a gender perspective, as geographical distribution and sex-disaggregated data are both crucial elements in effective planning and policymaking processes.

Two further additions have been made. The first is the inclusion of technical notes, which provide information on definitions and the methods of computation used to drive indicator values, thus providing users from different disciplines with transparent information that is in line with the United Nations Fundamental Principles of Official Statistics. The second innovation is the addition of a glossary of statistical terms.

Readers are encouraged to provide feedback and proposals for further enhancement of the Bulletin through the questionnaire provided. The electronic version of the Bulletin can be accessed on the ESCWA Statistics Division webpage at http://www.escwa.un.org/divisions/main.asp?division=sd.

ESCWA is grateful to member countries for their collaboration in producing the Bulletin. It also extends its appreciation to the United Nations Department of Economic and Social Affairs, New York, for its coordination and collaboration.

ومن العناصر الجديدة التي يتضمنها هذا العدد قائمة بتوفر البيانات، وهي قائمة مقارنة للمنطقة تبين مستوى القدرات الإحصائية في كل من البلدان الأعضاء. ويساعد تقييم هذه القائمة على معرفة مدى النقص في البيانات والتحسينات الواجب إجراؤها على المستوى الوطني. ويتضمن هذا العدد مجموعة من المؤشرات أوسع من تلك التي وردت في إعداد سابقة. كما أن الرسوم البيانية والنصوص التحليلية من شأنها تسهيل تفسير قيمة المؤشرات واتجاهاتها وبالتالي تلبية احتياجات أصحاب المصلحة على نحو أفضل. وبالإضافة إلى ذلك ترد البيانات، حيثما توفرت وحسب المقتضى، مصنفة بحسب التوزيع الجغرافي والنوع الاجتماعي، وهما عنصران لضمان الفعالية في التخطيط وصنع القرار.

وأضيف إلى هذا العدد أيضا مكونان آخران، الأول يتضمن المنهجية، وفيه معلومات عن تعاريف المصطلحات وطرق الاحتساب المستخدمة في استخلاص قيم المؤشرات، وبالتالي يزود المستخدمين على اختلاف مدارسهم بمعلومات شفافة تتسق مع مبادئ الأمم المتحدة الأساسية للإحصاءات الرسمية. والمكون الثاني هو مسرد بالمصطلحات الإحصائية.

ونأمل من القراء أن يرسلوا إلينا آراءهم ومقترحاتهم المرفقة بشأن إجراء مزيد من التحسين على النشرة من خلال ملء الاستبيان المرفق. ويمكن الاطلاع على النسخة الإلكترونية لهذه النشرة على موقع إدارة الإحصاء الخاصة بالإسكوا: http://www.escwa.un.org/divisions/main.asp?division=sd.

وتعرب الإسكوا عن شكرها للبلدان الأعضاء لتعاونها في إصدار هذه النشرة. كما توجه شكرها إلى إدارة الشؤون الاقتصادية والاجتماعية في الأمم المتحدة لما قامت به من تنسيق وتعاون.

DATA AVAILABILITY
توفر البيانات

Country	Population census	Births	Deaths	Foetal deaths	Infant deaths	Child deaths	Maternal mortality	Mean age at childbearing	Causes of death	Mean age at first marriage	Marriages	Divorces
Bahrain	■	■	■		■	■	■	■	■	■	■	■
Egypt	■	■	■	■	■	■	■	■	■	■	■	■
Iraq	■	■	■		■	■		■			■	
Jordan	■	■	■							■	■	■
Kuwait	■	■	■	■	■	■	■	■	■		■	■
Lebanon		■	■								■	■
Oman	■	■	■	■	■	■	■	■	■	■	■	
Palestine	■	■	■		■	■	■	■	■	■	■	■
Qatar	■	■	■	■	■	■	■	■	■	■	■	■
Saudi Arabia	■	■	■	■	■	■				■	■	■
Sudan	■	■										
Syrian Arab Republic	■	■	■								■	■
United Arab Emirates	■	■	■		■	■		■	■		■	■
Yemen	■	■	■								■	■

Criteria: A minimum of two data points are available.

الملحظة : توفر نقطتين من البيانات كحد أدنى.

x

الفصل الأول
Part I

السكان
Population

The population of the ESCWA region increases by 80.5 million in 17 years

The world population is currently growing by some 80 million per year, while in the ESCWA region total population estimates[1] reveal an increase of some 80.5 million between 1990 and 2007, representing an increase of almost 50 per cent in just 17 years. The increase in the ESCWA population is distributed almost equally between women and men.

Since 1990, Egypt, the Sudan and Iraq have had the largest populations in the ESCWA region. In this period, the population of Egypt has increased by over 20 million, that of the Sudan by almost 13 million and that of Iraq by over 10 million. However, their combined share of the total population of the region decreased from 63.8 per cent in 1990 to 60.5 per cent in 2007. This was primarily attributable to the significant decrease (3.4 percentage points) in Egypt's share of the total population of the region, the highest decrease in all member countries during the reporting period.

Of the 13 countries in the ESCWA region, six maintained their share or saw only a minimal (less than 0.2 per cent) change of share of the ESCWA total population during the period 1990-2007. The share in Bahrain, Kuwait, Lebanon, Oman, Qatar and Saudi Arabia has not changed since 1990. The highest increase of share was seen in Yemen (1.6 per cent between 1990 and 2007), the Yemeni population having increased by over 80 percentage points since 1990. Moreover, the share of both Palestine and the United Arab Emirates has increased by 0.74 per cent and 0.66 per cent respectively, predominantly as a result of the near doubling of the population in both countries during the reporting period.

Figures 1 and 2 illustrate the share of individual member countries as a percentage of total population of the ESCWA region in 1990 and 2007.

[1] United Nations. *World Population Prospects: The 2006 Revision* (ST/ESA/SER.A/261/ES). Available at: http://www.un.org/esa/desa.

سجّل عدد سكان منطقة الإسكوا زيادة بلغت ٨٠.٥ مليون نسمة في ١٧ سنة

يزداد عدد سكان العالم حاليا بمعدل ٨٠ مليون نسمة في السنة، بينما أظهرت تقديرات السكان[1] أن مجموع سكان منطقة الإسكوا سجل زيادة قدرها ٨٠.٥ مليون نسمة خلال الفترة من عام ١٩٩٠ إلى عام ٢٠٠٧، أي بمعدل ٥٠ في المائة في نحو ١٧ سنة. وتشكل الزيادة في عدد سكان منطقة الإسكوا نسبا متساوية من النساء والرجال.

ومنذ عام ١٩٩٠، سجلت أكبر زيادات في السكان في منطقة الإسكوا في مصر والسودان والعراق. فقد ازداد عدد السكان في مصر في تلك الفترة بأكثر من ٢٠ مليون نسمة، وفي السودان بنحو ١٣ مليون نسمة، وفي العراق بأكثر من ١٠ ملايين نسمة. ولكن الحصة المشتركة لهذه البلدان الثلاثة من مجموع سكان المنطقة انخفضت من ٦٣.٨ في المائة لعام ١٩٩٠ إلى ٦٠.٥ في المائة لعام ٢٠٠٧. ويعود هذا الانخفاض بشكل أساسي إلى الانخفاض الكبير في حصة مصر من مجموع سكان المنطقة والبالغ ٣.٤ في المائة، والذي يعتبر أكبر انخفاض شهدته البلدان الأعضاء في الفترة المشمولة بهذه الدراسة.

ومن بين البلدان الأعضاء في الإسكوا، حافظت ستة بلدان على حصتها أو لم تتغير حصة كل من البحرين، والكويت، ولبنان، وعُمان، وقطر، والمملكة العربية السعودية منذ عام ١٩٩٠، بينما سجلت حصة اليمن أعلى زيادة بلغت ١.٦ في المائة للزيادة التي بلغت ٨٠ في المائة في تلك الفترة. نظر للزيادة في عدد سكانه منذ عام ١٩٩٠. وشهدت حصة فلسطين والإمارات العربية المتحدة زيادة بنسبة ٠.٧٤ و٠.٦٦ في المائة على التوالي نتيجة تضاعف عدد السكان في كل من البلدين بمقدار الضعف في الفترة المشمولة بهذه الدراسة.

ويوضح الشكلان ١ و٢ حصة كل من البلدان الأعضاء كنسبة من مجموع سكان منطقة الإسكوا في عام ١٩٩٠ وعام ٢٠٠٧.

[1] الأمم المتحدة: التوقعات السكانية في العالم: تنقيح عام ٢٠٠٦ (ST/ESA/SER.A/261/ES). متوفر على الموقع التالي: http://www.un.org/esa/desa.

Figure 2. Country share in total population of the ESCWA region, 2007

الشكل ٢ - حصة البلدان من مجموع سكان منطقة الإسكوا لعام ٢٠٠٧

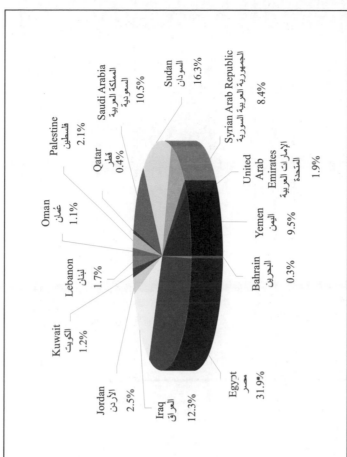

Figure 1. Country share in total population of the ESCWA region, 1990

الشكل ١ - حصة البلدان من مجموع سكان منطقة الإسكوا لعام ١٩٩٠

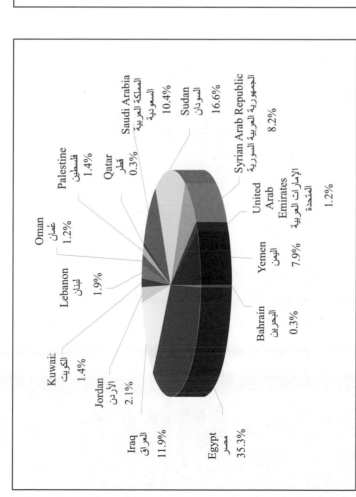

معدّلات النمو بلغت أكثر من ٣ في المائة سنوياً في معظم البلدان الأعضاء

في الفترة ١٩٩٥-١٩٩٠: سجّلت أعلى معدلات نمو في عدد السكان في كل من الأردن والإمارات العربية المتحدة (٥.٢ في المائة) واليمن: سجّلت أعلى معدلات نمو في عدد السكان في كل من الأردن (٥.٦ في المائة) والإمارات العربية المتحدة (٥.٣ في المائة) واليمن (٤.٦ في المائة). في الفترة ٢٠٠٠-١٩٩٥: سجّلت أعلى معدلات نمو في عدد السكان في كل من الكويت (٥.١ في المائة) والإمارات العربية المتحدة (٥.٨ في المائة). في الفترة ٢٠٠٥-٢٠٠٠: سجّلت أعلى معدلات النمو المتحدة... قطر (٥.١ في المائة) والإمارات العربية المتحدة (٤.٧ في المائة)... الكويت (٣.٨ في المائة) وفلسطين (٣.٥ في المائة) واليمن (٣.٠ في المائة) والأردن (٢.٩ في المائة). وتراوحت معدلات النمو السنوي للسكان في البلدان الأخرى بين ١.٨ و٢.٧ في المائة، باستثناء لبنان (١.٢ في المائة) وعُمان (٠.٨ في المائة).

وسجّلت أعلى معدلات انخفاض في نمو السكان في الأردن ولبنان وعُمان واليمن. وسُجّل انخفاض طفيف بلغ أقل من واحد في المائة في الفترة نفسها في البلدان الأخرى.

وتجدر الإشارة إلى أن الكويت سجّل معدلاً سالباً للنمو في عدد السكان (-٤.٣ في المائة) في الفترة ١٩٩٥-١٩٩٠، وفي المقابل سجّل الأردن أعلى معدل للنمو السكاني من الأردن خلال حرب الخليج الأولى. وفي الفترة ٢٠٠٠-١٩٩٥، شهد الكويت ارتفاعاً في معدل النمو السكاني وصل إلى (٥.١ في المائة)، بينما انخفض معدل النمو السكاني في الأردن في الفترة نفسها ليستقر عند ٢.٢ في المائة. ثم انخفض معدل النمو السنوي للسكان في الكويت أيضاً ليستقر عند ٣.٨ في المائة.

ويبين الشكل ٣ معدل النمو السنوي للسكان في البلدان الأعضاء في الإسكوا للفترتين ١٩٩٥-١٩٩٠ و٢٠٠٥-٢٠٠٠.

Growth rates over 3 per cent per year in almost all member countries

From 1990 to 1995, Jordan, the United Arab Emirates and Yemen recorded the highest population growth rates in the region at 5.6 per cent, 5.3 per cent and 4.6 per cent per year respectively. Both Kuwait (5.1 per cent per year) and the United Arab Emirates (5.8 per cent) recorded the highest population growth rates in 1995-2000, while Qatar (5.1 per cent) and the United Arab Emirates (4.7 per cent) had the highest growth rates in 2000-2005, followed by Kuwait (3.8 per cent), Palestine (3.5 per cent), Yemen (3.0 per cent) and Jordan (2.9 per cent). The population growth rate for the remaining countries ranged from 1.8 to 2.7 per cent per year, with the exception of Lebanon (1.2 per cent) and Oman (0.8 per cent).

Jordan, Lebanon, Oman and Yemen recorded the highest declines in population growth rates (over 2 percentage points) between 1990 and 2005. The remaining countries saw minimal declines of less than one percentage point in the same period.

It is worth noting that Kuwait had a negative population growth rate (-4.3 per cent) in 1990-1995, during which period Jordan conversely recorded the highest rate (5.6 per cent) in the region. This is directly attributable to the population exodus from Kuwait to Jordan during the first Gulf war. In 1995-2000, Kuwait subsequently witnessed a surge in growth rate, peaking at 5.1 per cent, while during the same period, the growth rate in Jordan fell, stabilizing at 2.2 per cent. The population growth rate in Kuwait in turn fell in 2000-2005, stabilizing at 3.8 per cent per year.

Figure 3 shows the average annual population growth rate for all ESCWA member countries for the periods 1990-1995 and 2000-2005.

Figure 3. Average annual population growth rate in ESCWA member countries, 1990-1995 and 2000-2005

الشكل ٣- معدل النمو السنوي للسكان في البلدان الأعضاء في الإسكوا، ٢٠٠٠-٢٠٠٥ و ١٩٩٠-١٩٩٥.

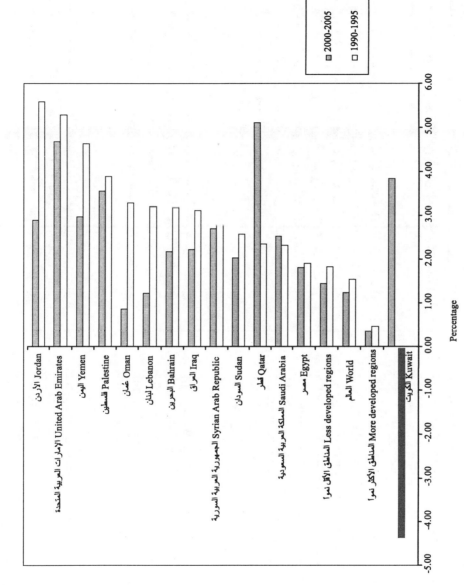

بحسب تقديرات عام ٢٠٠٦، بلغ معدل العمر المتوقع في الفترة ١٩٩٠-١٩٩٥ على الصعيد العالمي ٦٤.٢ سنة: ٦٦.٣ سنة للنساء و ٦٢.١ سنة للرجال. واليوم أصبح النساء والرجال على السواء يعيشون منذ ١٥ عاماً. ويبلغ معدل الزيادة في العمر المتوقع ٦. ١ سنة في المناطق الأكثر نمواً و ٢. ١ سنة في المناطق الأقل نمواً.

وحققت جميع البلدان الأعضاء في الإسكوا زيادات عالية في العمر المتوقع في الفترة ٢٠٠٥-١٩٩٠. وسجلت مصر الزيادة الأكبر وهي ٦. ١ سنة؛ وزاد العمر المتوقع ٤.٧ سنوات في اليمن، و ٤.٤ سنوات في قطر، و ٤. ١ سنوات في الإمارات العربية المتحدة، و ٣.٩ سنوات في الجمهورية العربية السورية، و ٢.٣ سنوات في الأردن، و ٣ سنوات في عمان، و ٢.٨ في كل من السودان والمملكة العربية السعودية، و ٢.٧ في فلسطين. وتحتل الإشارة إلى أن الكويت ولبنان حققا أدنى النسب في زيادة العمر المتوقع في المنطقة وهما ٧١ سنة و ٧٧ سنة على التوالي.

والاستثناء الوحيد لهذا الاتجاه التصاعد، حيث انخفض العمر المتوقع بمعدل ٢.٥ سنة للنساء والرجال. ويبلغ العمر المتوقع حالياً ٢.٩٥ سنة للنساء و ٥٧ سنة للرجال، أي بمعدل ٥. ٢ سنة للنساء و ٩.٥٤ سنة للرجال. ويعود ذلك بشكل أساسي إلى تدهور الخدمات والمرافق الصحية في العقد الأخير نتيجة للحرب والاضطرابات الداخلية.

ومن المتوقع أن يحقق معظم البلدان الأعضاء هدف الوصول إلى عمر متوقع يبلغ ٧٠ سنة بحلول عام ٢٠١٥، باستثناء العراق والسودان واليمن، الذين يُستبعد أن يحقق هذا الهدف بحلول عام ٢٠١٥ إلا إذا اتخذوا إجراءات استثنائية لتحسين نوعية حياة سكانهم.

وتبين الأشكال ٤ و ٥ و ٦ رسوماً مقارنة للعمر المتوقع عند الولادة في بعض البلدان الأعضاء في الإسكوا.

High gains in life expectancy achieved in the ESCWA region in the past 15 years

According to 2006 estimates, average life expectancy globally was 64.2 years: 66.3 years for women and 62.1 years for men in 1990-1995. Today, both women and men live approximately two years longer than 15 years ago: 1.6 years in the more developed regions and 2.1 years in the less developed regions.

All ESCWA member countries made substantial gains in life expectancy during the period 1990-2005. Egypt recorded the highest increase, with 6.1 years; in Yemen, life expectancy increased by 4.7 years; in Qatar, by 4.4 years; in the United Arab Emirates, by 4.1 years; in the Syrian Arab Republic, by 3.9 years; in Jordan, by 3.3 years; and in Oman, by 3.0 years. Life expectancy in both the Sudan and Saudi Arabia increased by 2.8 years, followed closely by Palestine with 2.7 years. It is worth noting that while Kuwait and Lebanon made the lowest gains during the reporting period, they have the highest life expectancy in the region, at 71 and 77 years respectively.

The sole exception to this upward trend is Iraq, where life expectancy has dropped by 2.5 years for both sexes; it currently stands at an average of 57 years: 59.3 years for women and 54.9 years for men. This is attributable in large part to the deterioration of health services and facilities in the last decade as a result of war and internal unrest.

Almost all member countries, with the exception of Iraq, the Sudan and Yemen, will reach the life expectancy target of 70 years by 2015. Iraq, the Sudan and Yemen, however, are highly unlikely to reach the target by 2015 unless they take exceptional measures to improve the quality of life of their people.

Figures 4, 5 and 6 provide a comparative illustration of life expectancy at birth in selected ESCWA member countries.

Figure 4. Life expectancy at birth, 1990-1995, 1995-2000 and 2000-2005 (total population)

الشكل ٤ – العمر المتوقع عند الولادة للجميع، ١٩٩٠–١٩٩٥ و٢٠٠٠–٢٠٠٥

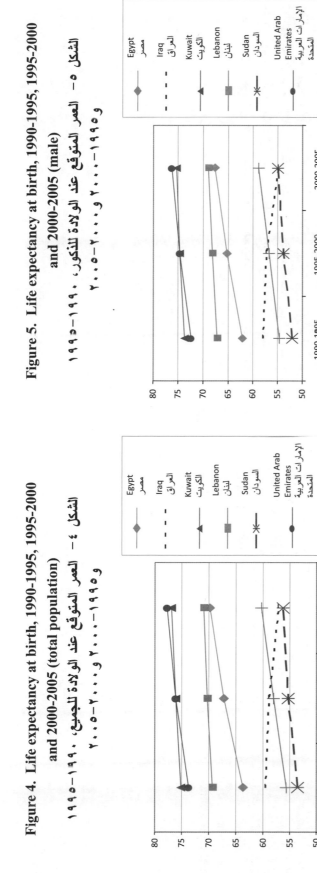

Figure 5. Life expectancy at birth, 1990-1995, 1995-2000 and 2000-2005 (male)

الشكل ٥ – العمر المتوقع عند الولادة للذكور، ١٩٩٠–١٩٩٥ و٢٠٠٠–٢٠٠٥

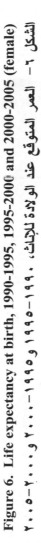

Figure 6. Life expectancy at birth, 1990-1995, 1995-2000 and 2000-2005 (female)

الشكل ٦ – العمر المتوقع عند الولادة للإناث، ١٩٩٠–١٩٩٥ و٢٠٠٠–٢٠٠٥

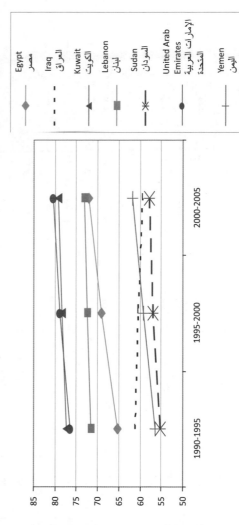

Census results reveal two clusters of population age structures

Almost all ESCWA member countries carry out a population census every 10 years, with the exception of Lebanon, where the last census was carried out in 1932. Almost all member countries undertook censuses between 2001 and 2007, with the exception of Iraq, where one is planned for 2009.

The traditional demographic balance in the Arab region has been based on a high fertility rate coupled with a high mortality rate. However, due to a rapid decline in infant mortality and an increase in life expectancy, the age structure of the population has changed in recent years and there has been a substantial increase in the number of people of working age (15-64 years). In addition to births and mortality, other processes, such as migration, have a strong influence on the age-sex structure of the population; this can clearly be identified in the shape of the population pyramid.

The population pyramid is a presentation of the age-sex distribution of the human population in a particular region. The countries of the ESCWA region can be categorized into two distinct clusters. The first comprises countries with large differences between the numbers of women and men: Bahrain, Kuwait, Oman, Qatar, Saudi Arabia and the United Arab Emirates. The male population of these countries is greater than the female population, particularly in the middle years (24-44 years). This difference is attributable to an increase in the number of non-nationals in the labour markets of the Gulf Cooperation Council (GCC) countries.

نتائج التعداد تبين عينين من الهياكل العمرية للسكان

يجري معظم البلدان الأعضاء في الإسكوا تعدادا للسكان كل عشر سنوات، باستثناء لبنان حيث أجري آخر تعداد للسكان في عام ١٩٣٢. وقد أجرى معظم البلدان التعداد في الفترة ما بين عامي ٢٠٠١ و٢٠٠٧، باستثناء العراق الذي من المقرر أن يجري التعداد في عام ٢٠٠٩.

وبستند التوازن الديمغرافي التقليدي في المنطقة العربية إلى معدلات عالية للخصوبة مقترنة بمعدلات عالية للوفيات. ولكن نتيجة للانخفاض السريع في وفيات الأطفال والارتفاع الكبير في العمر المتوقع، تغير الهيكل العمري للسكان بصورة كبيرة في السنوات الأخيرة وسُجّل ارتفاع كبير في عدد السكان بعمر العمل (١٥-٦٤ سنة). وبالإضافة إلى ولادات والوفيات، هناك عوامل أخرى، مثل الهجرة، لها أثر بالغ على التركيبة العمرية والنوع الاجتماعي للسكان تحديد ذلك بوضوح في شكل هرم سكاني من حيث العمر والنوع الاجتماعي.

ويمثل الهرم السكاني توزيع السكان في منطقة معينة بحسب مجموعتين من العمر والنوع. ويمكن تصنيف البلدان منطقة الإسكوا بحسب مجموعتين مختلفتين. فتتضمن المجموعة الأولى البلدان التي فيها فروق كبيرة بين أعداد النساء وأعداد الرجال، وهي: البحرين والكويت وعمان وقطر، والمملكة العربية السعودية، والإمارات العربية المتحدة. فعدد السكان الذكور في تلك البلدان يفوق عدد الإناث، وخصوصا في الأعمار المتوسطة (٢٤-٤٤ سنة). ويعود ذلك إلى زيادة عدد غير المواطنين في أسواق العمل في بلدان مجلس التعاون الخليجي.

Moreover, years of high fertility rates in the ESCWA region have resulted in a sizeable increase in the number of young people, giving the aggregate population pyramid a concave or bell shape, which is typical of developing countries. This can clearly be seen in the second cluster of countries, which have a large base and a narrow top: Egypt, Iraq, Jordan, Palestine, the Sudan, the Syrian Arab Republic and Yemen. The broad-based age structure of the population reflects the dual impact of high fertility and declines in mortality.

Many mothers from the previous generation are still producing large numbers of children, although according to the latest census data from a number of countries, the 0-4 years age group has been decreasing as a result of lower fertility rates. This is the case in Bahrain, Egypt, Oman, Saudi Arabia, the Sudan and Yemen, where the number of both girls and boys in this age group is smaller than the next age group (5-9 years).

The following country pyramids provide a clear illustration of age-sex distribution according to the latest census data.

وبالإضافة إلى ذلك، أدت معدلات الخصوبة المرتفعة لسنوات في منطقة الإسكوا إلى زيادة كبيرة في عدد السكان الشباب، مما جعل الهرم يتخذ شكل الجرس، وهو شكل نموذجي للبلدان النامية. وهذا ما يمكن ملاحظته في المجموعة الثانية من البلدان التي يتميز هرمها السكاني بقاعدة عريضة ورأس ضيق. وهذه البلدان هي: مصر، والعراق، والأردن، وفلسطين، والسودان، والجمهورية العربية السورية، واليمن. وتعكس القاعدة العريضة لهيكل السكان التأثير المزدوج لارتفاع معدلات الخصوبة وانخفاض معدلات الوفيات.

ولا يزال العديد من الأمهات اللواتي ينتمين إلى الجيل السابق يلدن أعداداً كبيرة من الأطفال، على الرغم من أن الفئة العمرية التي تتراوح أعمارها بين صفر إلى ٤ سنوات سجلت انخفاضاً نتيجة لانخفاض معدلات الخصوبة، وذلك بحسب بيانات التعدادات الأخيرة التي أجريت في عدد من البلدان. وهذه هي الحال في البحرين، ومصر، وعُمان، والمملكة العربية السعودية، واليمن، حيث يقل عدد الأطفال من تلك الفئة العمرية عن عدد الأطفال من الفئة العمرية ٥ إلى ٩ سنوات.

وتبين الأهرام السكانية التالية توزيع السكان بحسب العمر والنوع الاجتماعي وفقاً للبيانات المتوفرة في آخر تعداد.

وتبين الأهرام السكانية للبلدان فيما يلي رسماً واضحاً لتوزيع السكان بحسب العمر والنوع الاجتماعي وفقاً للبيانات المتوفرة في آخر تعداد.

٦

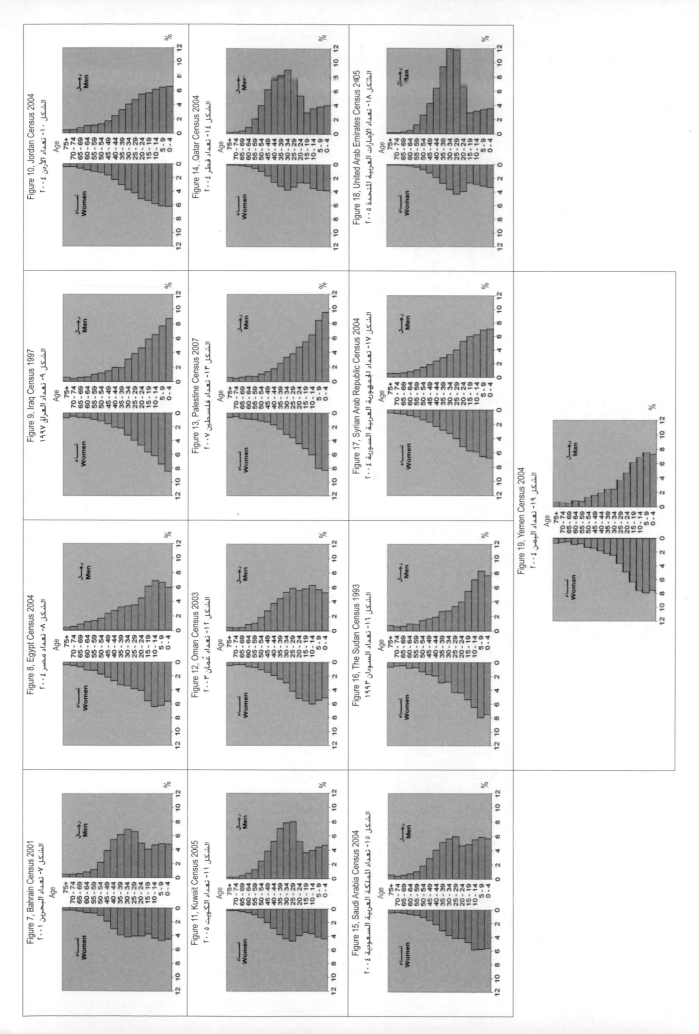

Figure 7, Bahrain Census 2001
الشكل ٧- تعداد البحرين ٢٠٠١

Figure 8, Egypt Census 2004
الشكل ٨- تعداد مصر ٢٠٠٤

Figure 9, Iraq Census 1997
الشكل ٩- تعداد العراق ١٩٩٧

Figure 10, Jordan Census 2004
الشكل ١٠- تعداد الأردن ٢٠٠٤

Figure 11, Kuwait Census 2005
الشكل ١١- تعداد الكويت ٢٠٠٥

Figure 12, Oman Census 2003
الشكل ١٢- تعداد عُمان ٢٠٠٣

Figure 13, Palestine Census 2007
الشكل ١٣- تعداد فلسطين ٢٠٠٧

Figure 14, Qatar Census 2004
الشكل ١٤- تعداد قطر ٢٠٠٤

Figure 15, Saudi Arabia Census 2004
الشكل ١٥- تعداد المملكة العربية السعودية ٢٠٠٤

Figure 16, The Sudan Census 1993
الشكل ١٦- تعداد السودان ١٩٩٣

Figure 17, Syrian Arab Republic Census 2004
الشكل ١٧- تعداد الجمهورية العربية السورية ٢٠٠٤

Figure 18, United Arab Emirates Census 2005
الشكل ١٨- تعداد الإمارات العربية المتحدة ٢٠٠٥

Figure 19, Yemen Census 2004
الشكل ١٩- تعداد اليمن ٢٠٠٤

10

TABLE 1. POPULATION ESTIMATES SINCE 1990

الجدول ١ – تقديرات السكان منذ عام ١٩٩٠

Country	1990	1995	2000	2001	2002	2003	2004	2005	2006	2007	البلد
Bahrain											**البحرين**
Men	256 249	336 552	374 164	382 175	390 557	399 116	407 550	415 643	423 341	430 723	رجال
Women	206 703	241 134	275 916	282 714	289 434	296 076	302 645	309 145	315 572	321 924	نساء
Total	**462 952**	**577 686**	**650 080**	**664 889**	**679 991**	**695 192**	**710 195**	**724 788**	**738 913**	**752 647**	**المجموع**
Egypt											**مصر**
Men	27 762 824	30 470 628	33 377 734	33 983 644	34 597 256	35 218 949	35 849 262	36 488 271	37 135 649	37 790 186	رجال
Women	27 374 129	30 177 670	33 150 844	33 773 785	34 406 509	35 048 915	35 700 756	36 361 522	37 030 647	37 707 728	نساء
Total	**55 136 953**	**60 648 298**	**66 528 578**	**67 757 429**	**69 003 765**	**70 267 864**	**71 550 018**	**72 849 793**	**74 166 296**	**75 497 914**	**المجموع**
Iraq											**العراق**
Men	9 377 894	10 956 321	12 688 907	13 007 631	13 313 986	13 607 416	13 887 946	14 157 149	14 412 026	14 656 456	رجال
Women	9 136 965	10 675 551	12 362 636	12 679 696	12 987 456	13 284 099	13 567 822	13 838 835	14 093 817	14 336 920	نساء
Total	**18 514 859**	**21 631 872**	**25 051 543**	**25 687 327**	**26 301 442**	**26 891 515**	**27 455 768**	**27 995 984**	**28 505 843**	**28 993 376**	**المجموع**
Jordan											**الأردن**
Men	1 695 507	2 250 003	2 479 869	2 538 360	2 606 512	2 683 398	2 766 731	2 854 350	2 947 308	3 045 233	رجال
Women	1 558 497	2 054 049	2 318 855	2 380 335	2 448 450	2 523 230	2 603 982	2 689 716	2 781 657	2 879 014	نساء
Total	**3 254 004**	**4 304 052**	**4 798 724**	**4 918 695**	**5 054 962**	**5 206 628**	**5 370 713**	**5 544 066**	**5 728 965**	**5 924 247**	**المجموع**
Kuwait											**الكويت**
Men	1 217 702	1 037 370	1 354 857	1 420 750	1 480 152	1 533 456	1 582 457	1 628 550	1 670 966	1 708 852	رجال
Women	0 925 301	0 687 630	0 873 505	0 917 942	0 959 122	0 997 472	1 034 546	1 071 450	1 107 684	1 142 292	نساء
Total	**2 143 003**	**1 725 000**	**2 228 362**	**2 338 692**	**2 439 274**	**2 530 928**	**2 617 003**	**2 700 000**	**2 778 650**	**2 851 144**	**المجموع**
Lebanon											**لبنان**
Men	1 449 093	1 718 792	1 848 075	1 870 928	1 894 535	1 918 538	1 942 146	1 964 805	1 986 577	2 007 843	رجال
Women	1 525 230	1 771 951	1 924 208	1 949 791	1 974 683	1 999 000	2 022 745	2 045 935	2 068 724	2 091 271	نساء
Total	**2 974 323**	**3 490 743**	**3 772 283**	**3 820 719**	**3 869 218**	**3 917 538**	**3 964 891**	**4 010 740**	**4 055 301**	**4 099 114**	**المجموع**
Oman											**عمان**
Men	1 025 901	1 280 662	1 391 694	1 396 481	1 396 413	1 395 044	1 397 024	1 405 661	1 422 477	1 446 579	رجال
Women	817 097	891 169	1 010 490	1 030 219	1 047 683	1 064 180	1 081 621	1 101 381	1 123 848	1 148 553	نساء
Total	**1 842 998**	**2 171 831**	**2 402 184**	**2 426 700**	**2 444 096**	**2 459 224**	**2 478 645**	**2 507 042**	**2 546 325**	**2 595 132**	**المجموع**
Palestine											**فلسطين**
Men	1 104 228	1 328 566	1 600 049	1 659 944	1 721 563	1 784 571	1 848 535	1 913 127	1 978 198	2 043 765	رجال
Women	1 050 240	1 288 595	1 549 398	1 606 509	1 665 433	1 725 801	1 787 081	1 848 878	1 911 069	1 973 731	نساء
Total	**2 154 468**	**2 617 161**	**3 149 447**	**3 266 453**	**3 386 996**	**3 510 372**	**3 635 616**	**3 762 005**	**3 889 267**	**4 017 496**	**المجموع**

TABLE 1 (*continued*)
الجدول ١ (تابع)

Country	1990	1995	2000	2001	2002	2003	2004	2005	2006	2007	البلد
Qatar											**قطر**
Men	313 170	346 280	400 425	424 127	452 674	483 126	511 400	534 588	551 569	563 253	رجال
Women	154 258	179 456	216 294	225 112	234 340	243 714	252 883	261 598	269 744	277 381	نساء
Total	**467 428**	**525 736**	**616 719**	**649 239**	**687 014**	**726 840**	**764 283**	**796 186**	**821 313**	**840 634**	**المجموع**
Saudi Arabia											**المملكة العربية السعودية**
Men	9 027 379	10 188 544	11 519 560	11 816 783	12 124 171	12 436 135	12 745 127	13 045 752	13 335 637	13 616 268	رجال
Women	7 228 364	8 062 039	9 287 029	9 540 542	9 792 275	10 044 677	10 301 845	10 566 608	10 839 303	11 118 264	نساء
Total	**16 255 743**	**18 250 583**	**20 806 589**	**21 357 325**	**21 916 446**	**22 480 812**	**23 046 972**	**23 612 360**	**24 174 940**	**24 734 532**	**المجموع**
Sudan											**السودان**
Men	13 025 915	14 826 513	16 776 821	17 138 996	17 488 360	17 835 420	18 195 004	18 577 505	18 986 719	19 418 643	رجال
Women	12 907 167	14 665 515	16 571 806	16 924 434	17 263 979	17 600 961	17 950 237	18 322 242	18 720 764	19 141 849	نساء
Total	**25 933 082**	**29 492 028**	**33 348 627**	**34 063 430**	**34 752 339**	**35 436 381**	**36 145 241**	**36 899 747**	**37 707 483**	**38 560 492**	**المجموع**
Syrian Arab Republic											**الجمهورية العربية السورية**
Men	6 411 726	7 369 771	8 333 037	8 555 040	8 788 885	9 032 739	9 283 670	9 538 979	9 798 828	10 062 344	رجال
Women	6 309 194	7 240 577	8 177 824	8 394 300	8 622 472	8 860 525	9 105 558	9 354 902	9 608 730	9 866 174	نساء
Total	**12 720 920**	**14 610 348**	**16 510 861**	**16 949 340**	**17 411 357**	**17 893 264**	**18 389 228**	**18 893 881**	**19 407 558**	**19 928 518**	**المجموع**
United Arab Emirates											**الإمارات العربية المتحدة**
Men	1 221 650	1 606 971	2 190 101	2 316 418	2 443 216	2 566 961	2 683 340	2 789 330	2 883 328	2 966 118	رجال
Women	645 433	824 562	1 057 118	1 107 950	1 159 715	1 211 877	1 263 792	1 314 961	1 365 148	1 414 321	نساء
Total	**1 867 083**	**2 431 533**	**3 247 219**	**3 424 368**	**3 602 931**	**3 778 838**	**3 947 132**	**4 104 291**	**4 248 476**	**4 380 439**	**المجموع**
Yemen											**اليمن**
Men	6 205 926	7 874 186	9 212 710	9 487 611	9 771 351	10 064 384	10 366 225	10 676 575	10 996 216	11 326 067	رجال
Women	6 107 650	7 648 773	8 969 023	9 242 139	9 523 280	9 813 113	10 111 694	10 419 104	10 736 031	11 063 105	نساء
Total	**12 313 576**	**15 522 959**	**18 181 733**	**18 729 750**	**19 294 631**	**19 877 497**	**20 477 919**	**21 095 679**	**21 732 247**	**22 389 172**	**المجموع**
ESCWA Region											**منطقة الإسكوا**
Men	80 125 164	91 591 159	103 548 003	105 998 888	108 469 631	110 959 253	113 466 417	115 990 285	118 528 839	121 082 330	رجال
Women	75 946 228	86 408 671	97 744 946	100 055 468	102 374 831	104 713 640	107 087 207	109 506 277	111 972 738	114 482 527	نساء
Total	**156 071 392**	**177 999 830**	**201 292 949**	**206 054 356**	**210 844 462**	**215 672 893**	**220 553 624**	**225 496 562**	**230 501 577**	**235 564 857**	**المجموع**

Source: United Nations, *World Population Prospects: The 2006 Revision.*

المصدر : الأمم المتحدة، التوقعات السكانية في العالم تنقيح عام ٢٠٠٦.

-12-

TABLE 2. AVERAGE ANNUAL RATE OF POPULATION CHANGE, 1990-1995, 1995-2000 AND 2000-2005

الجدول ٢ - معدل الزيادة السنوية للسكان، ١٩٩٠-١٩٩٥ و ١٩٩٥-٢٠٠٠ و ٢٠٠٠-٢٠٠٥

Country	Rate of change		معدل الزيادة	البلد
	1990-1995	1995-2000	2000-2005	
Bahrain	3.17	2.36	2.18	البحرين
Egypt	1.91	1.85	1.82	مصر
Iraq	3.11	2.94	2.22	العراق
Jordan	5.59	2.18	2.89	الأردن
Kuwait	-4.34	5.12	3.84	الكويت
Lebanon	3.20	1.55	1.23	لبنان
Oman	3.28	2.02	0.86	عمان
Palestine	3.89	3.70	3.56	فلسطين
Qatar	2.35	3.19	5.11	قطر
Saudi Arabia	2.32	2.62	2.53	المملكة العربية السعودية
Sudan	2.57	2.46	2.02	السودان
Syrian Arab Republic	2.77	2.45	2.70	الجمهورية العربية السورية
United Arab Emirates	5.28	5.79	4.69	الإمارات العربية المتحدة
Yemen	4.63	3.16	2.97	اليمن
World	1.54	1.37	1.24	العالم
More developed regions	0.45	0.32	0.36	البلدان الأكثر نمواً
Less developed regions	1.83	1.63	1.44	البلدان الأقل نمواً

Source: United Nations, *World Population Prospects: The 2006 Revision.*

المصدر : الأمم المتحدة، التوقعات السكانية في العالم : نتيجج عام ٢٠٠٦.

-13-

TABLE 3. LIFE EXPECTANCY AT BIRTH, 1990-1995, 1995-2000 AND 2000-2005

الجدول ٣- العمر المتوقع عند الولادة، ١٩٩٠-١٩٩٥ و ١٩٩٥-٢٠٠٠ و ٢٠٠٠-٢٠٠٥

Country	Life expectancy at birth 1990-1995			1995-2000			2000-2005		
	Total	Men	Women	Total	Men	Women	Total	Men	Women
	المجموع	رجال	نساء	المجموع	رجال	نساء	المجموع	رجال	نساء
Bahrain	72.6	71.1	74.8	73.9	72.5	75.8	74.8	73.5	76.5
Egypt	63.7	62.2	65.3	67.2	65.3	69.2	69.8	67.7	72.0
Iraq	59.5	58.0	61.1	58.8	57.3	60.4	57.0	54.9	59.3
Jordan	68.0	66.3	69.9	69.8	68.3	71.5	71.3	69.7	73.1
Kuwait	75.2	73.6	77.3	76.2	74.6	78.3	76.9	75.3	79.2
Lebanon	69.3	67.2	71.6	70.3	68.2	72.4	71.0	68.9	73.2
Oman	71.2	69.9	72.9	72.5	71.2	74.2	74.2	72.9	75.9
Palestine	69.7	68.1	71.4	71.1	69.4	72.7	72.4	70.8	73.9
Qatar	69.9	68.4	73.0	71.9	70.8	74.2	74.3	73.7	75.3
Saudi Arabia	68.8	67.4	70.8	70.5	68.9	72.7	71.6	69.8	74.0
Sudan	53.6	52.1	55.2	55.4	53.8	57.0	56.4	55.0	57.8
Syrian Arab Republic	69.2	67.6	71.2	71.5	69.7	73.4	73.1	71.2	74.9
United Arab Emirates	73.7	72.3	76.4	76.2	74.7	78.9	77.8	76.3	80.5
Yemen	55.6	54.7	56.5	58.0	56.8	59.3	60.3	58.8	61.8
World	64.2	62.1	66.3	65.2	63.0	67.4	66.0	63.9	68.3
More developed regions	74.0	70.2	77.8	74.8	71.1	78.5	75.6	72.0	79.3
Less developed regions	62.0	60.5	63.5	63.2	61.6	64.9	64.1	62.5	65.9

Source: United Nations, *World Population Prospects: The 2006 Revision.*

المصدر : الأمم المتحدة، التوقعات السكانية في العالم : نتيجة عام ٢٠٠٦.

البلد
البحرين
مصر
العراق
الأردن
الكويت
لبنان
عُمان
فلسطين
قطر
المملكة العربية السعودية
السودان
الجمهورية العربية السورية
الإمارات العربية المتحدة
اليمن
العالم
المناطق الأكثر نمواً
المناطق الأقل نمواً

العمر المتوقع عند الولادة

TABLE 4. POPULATION BY SEX, NATIONALITY AND RESIDENCE, LATEST AVAILABLE CENSUS

الجدول ٤ – السكان بحسب النوع الاجتماعي، والجنسية، ومكان الإقامة، آخر تعداد

Country	البلد	Census date تاريخ التعداد	Men رجال	Women نساء	Nationals مواطنون	Non-nationals غير مواطنين	Urban حضر	Rural ريف	Total المجموع
Bahrain	البحرين	2001	373 649	276 955	405 667	244 937	...	...	650 604
Egypt	مصر	2006	36 572 967	34 890 388	71 347 661	115 694	...	...	71 463 355
Iraq	العراق	1997	10 987 251	11 058 993	...	...	15 069 048	6 977 196	22 046 244
Jordan	الأردن	2004	2 626 287	2 477 352	4 711 366	392 273	3 997 383	1 106 256	5 103 639
Kuwait	الكويت	2005	1 310 067	903 336	880 774	1 332 629	...	...	2 213 403
Oman	عُمان	2003	1 313 239	1 027 576	1 781 558	559 257	1 673 480	667 335	2 340 815
Palestine	فلسطين	2007	1 911 957	1 855 170	...	...	...	...	3 767 127
Qatar	قطر	2004	496 382	247 647	...	...	...	...	744 029
Saudi Arabia	المملكة العربية السعودية	2004	12 557 240	10 121 022	16 527 340	6 150 922	...	...	22 678 262
Sudan	السودان	1993	10 671 615	10 595 025	...	...	6 794 263	14 472 377	21 266 640
Syrian Arab Republic	الجمهورية العربية السورية	2004	9 197	8 724	...	...	9 588	8 333	17 921
United Arab Emirates	الإمارات العربية المتحدة	2005	2 806 152	1 300 275	825 495	3 280 932	3 384 839	721 588	4 106 427
Yemen	اليمن	2004	10 036 953	9 648 208	19 597 290	87 871	...	...	19 685 161

TABLE 5. POPULATION OF BAHRAIN BY AGE GROUP, 2001 CENSUS
الجدول ٥ - السكان في البحرين بحسب الفئة العمرية، تعداد ٢٠٠١

Age group الفئة العمرية	Nationals مواطنين		Non-nationals غير مواطنين		Urban حضر		Rural ريف		Total المجموع	
	Men رجال	Women نساء	Men رجال	Women نساء	Men رجال	Women نساء	Men رجال	Women نساء	Men رجال	Women نساء
<1	4 827	4 434	1 191	1 033	...	...	...	...	6 018	5 467
1-4	19 878	19 182	5 058	4 782	...	...	...	...	24 936	23 964
5-9	25 666	25 059	5 802	5 623	...	...	...	...	31 468	30 682
10-14	25 281	23 879	5 033	4 641	...	...	...	...	30 314	28 520
15-19	22 729	21 511	3 603	3 152	...	...	...	...	26 332	24 663
20-24	19 681	18 677	12 482	7 835	...	...	...	...	32 163	26 512
25-29	15 303	14 957	27 526	11 589	...	...	...	...	42 829	26 546
30-34	13 942	14 635	30 823	12 889	...	...	...	...	44 765	27 524
35-39	14 039	15 298	25 882	10 196	...	...	...	...	39 921	25 494
40-44	11 816	12 936	23 619	6 887	...	...	...	...	35 435	19 823
45-49	9 489	8 893	15 522	3 873	...	...	...	...	25 011	12 766
50-54	6 573	5 468	7 521	1 769	...	...	...	...	14 094	7 237
55-59	4 198	4 358	2 939	761	...	...	...	...	7 137	5 119
60-64	3 822	4 172	1 115	392	...	...	...	...	4 937	4 564
65-69	2 705	3 027	448	221	...	...	...	...	3 153	3 243
70-74	2 220	2 259	276	124	...	...	...	...	2 496	2 383
75+	2 454	2 299	186	144	...	...	...	...	2 640	2 443
Not stated غير محدد	0	0	0	0	...	...	...	...	...	...
Total المجموع	204 623	201 044	169 026	75 911	...	...	...	...	373 649	276 955

TABLE 6. POPULATION OF EGYPT BY AGE GROUP, 2006 CENSUS

الجدول ٦ - السكان في مصر بحسب الفئة العمرية، تعداد ٢٠٠٦

Age group الفئة العمرية	Nationals مواطنين		Non-nationals غير مواطنين		Urban حضر		Rural ريف		Total المجموع	
	Men رجال	Women نساء	Men رجال	Women نساء	Men رجال	Women نساء	Men رجال	Women نساء	Men رجال	Women نساء
<1	4 231 397	4 024 007	4 214	3 850	…	…	…	…	4 235 611	4 027 857
1-4	4 744 139	4 437 825	4 427	4 012	…	…	…	…	4 748 566	4 441 837
5-9	4 908 718	4 559 117	4 574	4 338	…	…	…	…	4 913 292	4 563 455
10-14	4 344 315	3 975 933	5 759	4 740	…	…	…	…	4 350 074	3 980 673
15-19	3 175 297	2 903 359	8 978	6 143	…	…	…	…	3 184 275	2 909 502
20-24	2 517 666	2 731 447	6 517	5 337	…	…	…	…	2 524 183	2 736 784
25-29	2 405 265	2 419 374	6 218	5 351	…	…	…	…	2 411 483	2 424 725
30-34	2 297 883	2 317 903	5 030	4 175	…	…	…	…	2 302 913	2 322 078
35-39	1 932 096	1 889 329	4 896	3 602	…	…	…	…	1 936 992	1 892 931
40-44	1 675 757	1 539 636	3 810	2 712	…	…	…	…	1 679 567	1 542 348
45-49	1 202 176	1 225 326	3 567	2 296	…	…	…	…	1 205 743	1 227 622
50-54	947 728	839 476	2 322	1 495	…	…	…	…	950 050	840 971
55-59	845 859	832 166	1 814	1 332	…	…	…	…	847 673	833 498
60-64	611 359	508 973			…	…	…	…		
65-69	377 776	357 159			…	…	…	…		
70-74	291 168	278 032	2 242	1 943	…	…	…	…	1 282 545	1 146 107
75+					…	…	…	…		
Not stated غير محدد	0	0	0	0	…	…	…	…	0	0
Total المجموع	36 508 599	34 839 062	64 368	51 326	…	…	…	…	36 572 967	34 890 388

TABLE 7. POPULATION OF IRAQ BY AGE GROUP, 1997 CENSUS
الجدول ٧- السكان في العراق بحسب الفئة العمرية، تعداد ١٩٩٧

Age group / الفئة العمرية	Nationals / مواطنون Men / رجال	Nationals Women / نساء	Non-nationals / غير مواطنين Men / رجال	Non-nationals Women / نساء	Urban / حضر Men / رجال	Urban Women / نساء	Rural / ريف Men / رجال	Rural Women / نساء	Total / المجموع Men / رجال	Total Women / نساء
<1	...	...	...	...	1 218 197	1 188 647	693 650	678 488	1 911 847	1 867 135
1-4	...	...	...	...	1 124 600	1 087 118	567 526	544 208	1 692 126	1 631 326
5-9	...	...	...	...	955 442	918 804	469 604	448 068	1 425 046	1 366 872
10-14	...	...	...	...	883 604	846 938	409 832	399 830	1 293 436	1 246 768
15-19	...	...	...	...	713 054	706 362	306 213	322 115	1 019 267	1 028 477
20-24	...	...	...	...	591 288	606 625	258 096	268 456	849 384	875 081
25-29	...	...	...	...	499 004	509 079	181 806	201 197	680 810	710 275
30-34	...	...	...	...						
35-39	...	...	...	...	327 146	359 495	86 760	126 752	413 906	486 247
40-44	...	...	...	...	316 790	323 836	112 632	130 766	429 422	454 602
45-49	...	...	...	...	239 218	244 225	88 217	106 065	327 435	350 250
50-54	...	...	...	...	197 065	184 976	66 790	71 642	263 855	256 618
55-59	...	...	...	...	162 203	153 921	52 862	55 215	215 065	209 156
60-64	...	...	...	...	99 247	113 184	35 597	43 538	134 844	156 722
65-69	...	...	...	...	86 028	103 180	37 398	43 858	123 426	147 038
70-74	...	...	...	...	53 298	75 045	28 715	36 055	82 013	111 130
75-79	...	...	...	...	33 861	45 496	21 254	23 459	55 115	68 955
80-84	...	...	...	...	42 465	59 607	27 789	32 743	70 254	92 350
Not stated / غير محدد	...	...	...	...	0	0	0	0	0	0
Total / المجموع	...	...	...	...	7 542 510	7 526 538	3 444 741	3 532 455	10 987 251	11 058 993

-18-

TABLE 8. POPULATION OF JORDAN BY AGE GROUP, 2004 CENSUS
الجدول ٨ - السكان في الأردن بحسب الفئة العمرية، تعداد ٢٠٠٤

Age group القئة العمرية	Nationals مواطنون		Non-nationals غير مواطنين		Urban حضر		Rural ريف		Total المجموع	
	Men رجال	Women نساء	Men رجال	Women نساء	Men رجال	Women نساء	Men رجال	Women نساء	Men رجال	Women نساء
<1	59 102	56 690	3 541	3 424	48 529	46 445	14 114	13 669	62 643	60 114
1-4	255 676	242 727	14 897	14 274	209 140	199 753	61 433	57 248	270 573	257 001
5-9	313 300	298 550	15 833	15 188	253 774	241 809	75 359	71 929	329 133	313 738
10-14	298 669	283 693	14 414	13 353	240 723	223 598	72 360	68 448	313 083	297 046
15-19	270 699	257 522	16 994	14 623	221 213	210 062	66 480	62 083	287 693	272 145
20-24	248 508	232 933	31 092	27 660	217 092	204 308	62 508	56 285	279 600	260 593
25-29	202 463	193 959	37 311	22 528	186 570	169 380	53 204	47 107	239 774	216 487
30-34	174 537	175 223	32 641	16 768	164 238	151 997	42 940	39 994	207 178	191 991
35-39	145 100	145 613	22 637	10 076	134 829	124 907	32 908	30 782	167 737	155 689
40-44	108 609	111 054	15 336	6 401	101 442	95 481	22 503	21 974	123 945	117 455
45-49	78 163	79 165	8 935	4 193	70 890	67 482	16 208	15 876	87 098	83 358
50-54	58 488	60 234	6 119	3 399	51 210	50 969	13 397	12 664	64 607	63 633
55-59	51 589	55 163	4 176	2 793	45 618	47 275	10 147	10 681	55 765	57 956
60-64	49 252	44 722	2 832	1 981	42 634	37 635	9 450	9 068	52 084	46 703
65-69	35 497	33 430	1 598	1 298	29 956	27 528	7 139	7 200	37 095	34 728
70-74	22 574	22 447	893	906	18 503	18 455	4 964	4 898	23 467	23 353
75-79	12 215	11 168	436	449	9 923	9 237	2 728	2 380	12 651	11 617
80+	9 844	11 463	293	460	7 369	9 007	2 768	2 916	10 137	11 923
Not stated غير محدد	662	663	1362	1159	1778	1624	246	198	2024	1822
Total المجموع	2 394 947	2 316 419	231 340	160 933	2 055 431	1 941 952	570 856	535 400	2 626 287	2 477 352

TABLE 9. POPULATION OF KUWAIT BY AGE GROUP, 2005 CENSUS

الجدول ٩ – السكان في الكويت بحسب الفئة العمرية، تعداد ٢٠٠٥

Age group الفئة العمرية	Nationals مواطنون Men رجال	Nationals Women نساء	Non-nationals غير مواطنين Men رجال	Non-nationals Women نساء	Urban حضر Men رجال	Urban Women نساء	Rural ريف Men رجال	Rural Women نساء	Total المجموع Men رجال	Total Women نساء
<1	60 353	56 847	42 356	39 083	...	...	...	...	102 709	95 930
1-4	60 431	56 158	36 575	34 294	...	...	...	...	97 006	90 452
5-9	56 025	52 688	30 302	27 178	...	...	...	...	86 327	79 856
10-14	49 580	47 967	30 749	26 821	...	...	...	...	80 329	74 788
15-19	40 151	39 310	73 314	46 368	...	...	...	...	113 465	85 678
20-24	31 029	33 255	144 236	69 913	...	...	...	...	175 265	103 168
25-29	27 283	30 086	144 145	65 768	...	...	...	...	171 428	95 854
30-34	24 429	27 392	129 609	55 125	...	...	...	...	154 038	82 517
35-39	20 795	23 341	93 682	38 841	...	...	...	...	114 477	62 182
40-44	15 733	19 674	68 682	24 040	...	...	...	...	84 415	43 714
45-49	11 855	14 881	41 814	13 014	...	...	...	...	53 669	27 895
50-54	5 202	11 143	22 031	6 848	...	...	...	...	27 233	17 991
55-59	6 876	7 953	9 586	3 685	...	...	...	...	16 462	11 538
60-64	5 712	5 581	4 257	2 127	...	...	...	...	9 969	7 708
65-69	3 294	3 356	1 770	1 295	...	...	...	...	5 064	4 551
70-74	2 034	1 800	697	689	...	...	...	...	2 731	2 489
75-79	892	948	272	347	...	...	...	...	1 164	1 295
80-84	673	652	238	269	...	...	...	...	911	921
85+					...	...	...	...		
Not stated غير محدد	8 630	13 765	1 775	834	...	...	...	...	10 405	14 599
Total المجموع	433 977	446 797	876 090	456 539	...	...	...	...	1 310 067	903 336

-20-

TABLE 10. POPULATION OF OMAN BY AGE GROUP, 2003 CENSUS

الجدول ١٠- السكان في عُمان بحسب الفئة العمرية، تعداد ٢٠٠٣

Age group القئة العمرية	Nationals مواطنين Men رجال	Nationals مواطنين Women نساء	Non-nationals غير مواطنين Men رجال	Non-nationals غير مواطنين Women نساء	Urban حضر Men رجال	Urban حضر Women نساء	Rural ريف Men رجال	Rural ريف Women نساء	Total Men رجال	Total Women نساء
<1	21 884	21 601	2 392	2 313	83 774 [*]	80 886 [*]	39 598 [*]	38 499 [*]	24 276	23 914
1-4	87 659	84 385	11 437	11 086	—	—	—	—	99 096	95 471
5-9	121 220	116 256	12 137	11 309	88 659	84 180	44 698	43 385	133 357	127 565
10-14	137 621	132 644	9 620	8 335	97 801	93 422	49 440	47 557	147 241	140 979
15-19	130 466	124 741	6 082	5 467	93 894	87 920	42 654	42 288	136 548	130 208
20-24	107 482	106 778	23 493	15 013	96 847	89 323	34 128	32 468	130 975	121 791
25-29	74 032	74 227	64 195	23 027	105 365	74 232	32 862	23 022	138 227	97 254
30-34	47 499	45 276	77 107	23 989	97 306	54 689	27 300	14 576	124 606	69 265
35-39	35 741	37 347	68 399	18 972	81 623	43 348	22 517	12 971	104 140	56 319
40-44	29 449	31 527	59 122	12 511	69 905	33 050	18 666	10 988	88 571	44 038
45-49	23 715	26 839	40 523	6 626	50 116	24 188	14 122	9 277	64 238	33 465
50-54	20 383	22 312	23 406	3 535	33 611	17 967	10 178	7 880	43 789	25 847
55-59	15 935	15 203	8 707	1 732	17 948	11 508	6 694	5 427	24 642	16 935
60-64	17 240	14 808	3 485	1 067	13 643	10 350	7 082	5 525	20 725	15 875
65-69	10 389	7 989	1 074	617	7 315	5 571	4 148	3 035	11 463	8 606
70-74	8 959	7 973	588	413	5 815	5 257	3 732	3 129	9 547	8 386
75-79	3 852	3 534	238	220	2 453	2 371	1 637	1 383	4 090	3 754
80-84	3 611	3 914	141	118	2 128	2 420	1 624	1 612	3 752	4 032
85+	3 191	3 501	128	81	1 843	2 150	1 476	1 432	3 319	3 582
Not stated غير محدد	212	163	425	127	425	177	212	113	637	290
Total المجموع	900 540	881 018	412 699	146 558	950 471	723 009	362 768	304 567	1 313 239	1 027 576

[*] In the Urban/Rural columns the <1 and 1–4 age groups appear combined in the first data value.

-21-

TABLE 11. POPULATION OF PALESTINE BY AGE GROUP, 2007 CENSUS*
الجدول ١١- السكان في فلسطين بحسب الفئة العمرية، تعداد ٢٠٠٧ (*)

Age group الفئة العمرية	Nationals مواطنين Men رجال	Women نساء	Non-nationals غير مواطنين Men رجال	Women نساء	Urban حضر Men رجال	Women نساء	Rural ريف Men رجال	Women نساء	Total Men رجال	Women نساء
<1	…	…	…	…	…	…	…	…	…	…
1-4	…	…	…	…	…	…	…	…	302 905	290 544
5-9	…	…	…	…	…	…	…	…	276 802	265 674
10-14	…	…	…	…	…	…	…	…	254 693	244 299
15-19	…	…	…	…	…	…	…	…	219 408	210 992
20-24	…	…	…	…	…	…	…	…	169 381	160 787
25-29	…	…	…	…	…	…	…	…	138 971	134 482
30-34	…	…	…	…	…	…	…	…	117 446	115 277
35-39	…	…	…	…	…	…	…	…	98 469	94 780
40-44	…	…	…	…	…	…	…	…	87 006	80 511
45-49	…	…	…	…	…	…	…	…	66 646	61 472
50-54	…	…	…	…	…	…	…	…	45 578	44 473
55-59	…	…	…	…	…	…	…	…	33 761	32 836
60-64	…	…	…	…	…	…	…	…	23 554	27 545
65-69	…	…	…	…	…	…	…	…	15 997	21 505
70-74	…	…	…	…	…	…	…	…	13 653	17 763
75-79	…	…	…	…	…	…	…	…	9 426	13 180
80+	…	…	…	…	…	…	…	…	8 888	11 692
Not stated غير محدد	…	…	…	…	…	…	…	…	29 372	27 357
Total المجموع	…	…	…	…	…	…	…	…	1 911 957	1 855 170

* Includes population counted during the period 1-16 December 2007 and uncounted population estimates according to post-enumeration survey.

(*) يشمل السكان الذين تم عدّهم خلال الفترة ١-١٦ كانون الأول/ديسمبر ٢٠٠٧ وتقديرات السكان الذين لم يتم عدّهم، وفقا للاستقصاء اللاحق لعملية العد.

TABLE 12. POPULATION OF QATAR BY AGE GROUP, 2004 CENSUS

الجدول ١٢ - السكان في قطر بحسب الفئة العمرية، تعداد ٢٠٠٤

Age group القئة العمرية	Nationals مواطنون		Non-nationals غير مواطنين		Urban حضر		Rural ريف		Total المجموع	
	Men رجال	Women نساء	Men رجال	Women نساء	Men رجال	Women نساء	Men رجال	Women نساء	Men رجال	Women نساء
<1	5 847	5 708	...	...	...	...	...	...	...	...
1-4	24 212	22 781	...	...	...	...	...	...	...	...
5-9	28 420	27 814	...	...	...	...	...	...	...	...
10-14	26 687	26 149	...	...	...	...	...	...	...	...
15-19	22 187	20 004	...	...	...	...	...	...	...	...
20-24	39 896	19 671	...	...	...	...	...	...	...	...
25-29	59 477	24 576	...	...	...	...	...	...	...	...
30-34	66 976	27 833	...	...	...	...	...	...	...	...
35-39	61 624	23 773	...	...	...	...	...	...	...	...
40-44	56 617	19 260	...	...	...	...	...	...	...	...
45-49	46 488	12 631	...	...	...	...	...	...	...	...
50-54	29 738	7 615	...	...	...	...	...	...	...	...
55-59	15 771	4 104	...	...	...	...	...	...	...	...
60-64	6 768	2 359	...	...	...	...	...	...	...	...
65-69	2 805	1 504	...	...	...	...	...	...	...	...
70-74	1 619	925	...	...	...	...	...	...	...	...
75-79	676	470	...	...	...	...	...	...	...	...
80+	574	470	...	...	...	...	...	...	...	...
Not stated غير محدد	0	0	...	...	...	...	...	...	...	...
Total المجموع	496 382	247 647	...	...	...	...	...	...	...	...

TABLE 13. POPULATION OF SAUDI ARABIA BY AGE GROUP, 2004 CENSUS
الجدول ١٣ – السكان في المملكة العربية السعودية بحسب الفئة العمرية، تعداد ٢٠٠٤

Age group الفئة العمرية	Nationals مواطنين		Non-nationals غير مواطنين		Urban حضر		Rural ريف		Total المجموع	
	Men رجال	Women نساء	Men رجال	Women نساء	Men رجال	Women نساء	Men رجال	Women نساء	Men رجال	Women نساء
<1	210 963	206 990	41 790	39 991	…	…	…	…	252 753	246 981
1-4	855 047	847 535	181 591	175 756	…	…	…	…	1 036 638	1 023 291
5-9	1 127 253	1 112 582	207 007	197 901	…	…	…	…	1 334 260	1 310 483
10-14	1 081 884	1 155 728	176 568	167 659	…	…	…	…	1 258 452	1 323 387
15-19	948 707	938 982	150 298	142 200	…	…	…	…	1 099 005	1 081 182
20-24	760 146	786 510	298 251	159 920	…	…	…	…	1 058 397	946 430
25-29	725 413	701 326	626 706	240 156	…	…	…	…	1 352 119	941 482
30-34	569 152	575 126	709 730	271 093	…	…	…	…	1 278 882	846 219
35-39	492 543	498 170	674 734	190 103	…	…	…	…	1 167 277	688 273
40-44	411 890	372 981	511 983	121 907	…	…	…	…	923 873	494 888
45-49	313 340	277 511	338 148	72 775	…	…	…	…	651 488	350 286
50-54	222 166	199 415	193 133	43 516	…	…	…	…	415 299	242 931
55-59	146 079	153 194	84 880	21 644	…	…	…	…	230 959	174 838
60-64	126 594	134 390	39 555	14 973	…	…	…	…	166 149	149 363
65-69	103 245	101 213	16 678	7 846	…	…	…	…	119 923	109 059
70-74	77 277	84 898	9 837	6 381	…	…	…	…	87 114	91 279
75-79	49 598	37 629	4 193	2 767	…	…	…	…	53 791	40 396
80+	66 073	55 790	4 788	4 464	…	…	…	…	70 861	60 254
Not stated غير محدد	0	0	0	0	…	…	…	…	0	0
Total المجموع	8 287 370	8 239 970	4 269 870	1 881 052	…	…	…	…	12 557 240	10 121 022

-24-

TABLE 14. POPULATION OF THE SUDAN BY AGE GROUP, 1993 CENSUS

الجدول ١٤ – السكان في السودان بحسب الفئة العمرية، تعداد ١٩٩٣

Age group الفئة العمرية	Nationals مواطنين		Non-nationals غير مواطنين		Urban حضر		Rural ريف		Total المجموع	
	Men رجال	Women نساء	Men رجال	Women نساء	Men رجال	Women نساء	Men رجال	Women نساء	Men رجال	Women نساء
<1	…	…	…	…	454 369	439 215	1169 733	1148 692	1624 102	1587 907
1-4	…	…	…	…	467 702	456 925	1 296 421	1 229 339	1 764 123	1 686 264
5-9	…	…	…	…	427 856	404 336	1 079 671	962 681	1 507 527	1 367 017
10-14	…	…	…	…	411 410	382 512	754 105	752 599	1 165 515	1 135 111
15-19	…	…	…	…	385 865	338 926	466 392	593 414	852 257	932 340
20-24	…	…	…	…	310 804	311 201	405 617	606 510	716 421	917 711
25-29	…	…	…	…	257 706	196 196	332 792	397 917	590 498	594 113
30-34	…	…	…	…	223 250	198 560	344 459	426 488	567 709	625 048
35-39	…	…	…	…	145 782	121 294	257 873	288 168	403 655	409 462
40-44	…	…	…	…	128 957	114 400	227 184	249 621	356 141	364 021
45-49	…	…	…	…	98 743	85 205	204 580	201 631	303 323	286 836
50-54	…	…	…	…	62 582	50 706	125 486	107 179	188 068	157 885
55-59	…	…	…	…	60 257	50 241	143 798	125 094	204 055	175 335
60-64	…	…	…	…	38 522	30 974	97 007	70 066	135 529	101 040
65-69	…	…	…	…	30 959	29 500	90 845	79 096	121 804	108 596
70-74	…	…	…	…	37 408	35 409	117 761	105 066	155 169	140 475
75+	…	…	…	…	4 612	1 879	11 107	3 985	15 719	5 864
Not stated غير محدد	…	…	…	…						
Total المجموع	…	…	…	…	3 546 784	3 247 479	7 124 831	7 347 546	10 671 615	10 595 025

TABLE 15. POPULATION OF THE SYRIAN ARAB REPUBLIC BY AGE GROUP, 2004 CENSUS

الجدول ١٥ – السكان في الجمهورية العربية السورية بحسب الفئة العمرية، تعداد ٢٠٠٤

Age group الفئة العمرية	Nationals مواطنين		Non-nationals غير مواطنين		Urban حضر		Rural ريف		Total المجموع	
	Men رجال	Women نساء	Men رجال	Women نساء	Men رجال	Women نساء	Men رجال	Women نساء	Men رجال	Women نساء
<1	226 000	214 000	...	...	112 000	106 000	114 000	108 000	226 000	214 000
1-4	1 047 000	989 000	...	...	532 000	503 000	515 000	486 000	1 047 000	989 000
5-9	1 235 000	1 164 000	...	...	633 000	596 000	602 000	568 000	1 235 000	1 164 000
10-14	1 114 000	1 040 000	...	...	578 000	539 000	536 000	501 000	1 114 000	1 040 000
15-19	1 078 000	1 023 000	...	...	560 000	532 000	518 000	491 000	1 078 000	1 023 000
20-24	948 000	916 000	...	...	504 000	486 000	444 000	430 000	948 000	916 000
25-29	727 000	709 000	...	...	393 000	380 000	334 000	329 000	727 000	709 000
30-34	597 000	583 000	...	...	335 000	325 000	262 000	258 000	597 000	583 000
35-39	516 000	500 000	...	...	296 000	284 000	220 000	216 000	516 000	500 000
40-44	427 000	409 000	...	...	259 000	240 000	168 000	169 000	427 000	409 000
45-49	327 000	307 000	...	...	198 000	178 000	129 000	129 000	327 000	307 000
50-54	269 000	249 000	...	...	159 000	137 000	110 000	112 000	269 000	249 000
55-59	189 000	172 000	...	...	109 000	96 000	80 000	76 000	189 000	172 000
60-64	150 000	146 000	...	...	85 000	78 000	65 000	68 000	150 000	146 000
65-69	111 000	101 000	...	...	62 000	54 000	49 000	47 000	111 000	101 000
70-74	103 000	92 000	...	...	52 000	46 000	51 000	46 000	103 000	92 000
75-79	54 000	41 000	...	...	26 000	22 000	28 000	19 000	54 000	41 000
80+	47 000	39 000	...	...	20 000	19 000	27 000	20 000	47 000	39 000
Not stated غير محدد	32 000	30 000	...	...	28 000	26 000	4 000	4 000	32 000	30 000
Total المجموع	9 197 000	8 724 000	...	...	4 941 000	4 647 000	4 256 000	4 077 000	9 197 000	8 724 000

TABLE 16. POPULATION OF THE UNITED ARAB EMIRATES BY AGE GROUP, 2005 CENSUS
الجدول ١٦ - السكان في الإمارات العربية المتحدة بحسب الفئة العمرية، تعداد ٢٠٠٥

Age group القئة العمرية	Nationals مواطنون		Non-nationals غير مواطنين		Urban حضر		Rural ريف		Total المجموع	
	Men رجال	Women نساء	Men رجال	Women نساء	Men رجال	Women نساء	Men رجال	Women نساء	Men رجال	Women نساء
<1 / 1-4	55 120	52 310	90 497	84 217	115 800	108 369	29 801	28 169	145 617	136 527
5-9	52 371	49 704	87 567	79 754	111 645	102 170	28 284	27 283	139 938	129 458
10-14	53 985	50 382	76 777	67 887	101 461	90 889	29 317	27 390	130 762	118 269
15-19	55 575	52 536	65 823	58 304	91 065	82 127	30 323	28 711	121 398	110 840
20-24	50 673	52 764	221 350	108 756	222 387	126 692	49 649	34 838	272 023	161 520
25-29	39 396	41 121	444 220	137 028	410 228	148 462	73 429	29 675	483 616	178 149
30-34	25 846	26 497	464 072	123 994	417 909	130 590	71 970	19 892	489 918	150 491
35-39	20 189	21 554	366 565	92 265	329 059	98 409	57 703	15 435	386 754	113 819
40-44	14 633	16 366	248 093	62 190	220 959	67 833	41 759	10 710	262 726	78 556
45-49	12 433	13 857	162 043	37 458	145 298	43 434	29 161	7 877	174 476	51 315
50-54	10 246	9 947	97 081	21 592	89 983	26 536	17 356	5 003	107 327	31 539
55-59	7 893	6 341	43 410	9 467	42 788	13 022	8 515	2 782	51 303	15 808
60-64	6 176	4 549	12 632	3 971	15 510	6 647	3 310	1 880	18 808	8 520
65-69	5 335	3 283	3 840	2 001	6 623	3 892	2 549	1 393	9 175	5 284
70-74	3 657	2 699	1 746	1 319	3 659	2 762	1 732	1 251	5 403	4 018
75-79	1 621	1 205	576	622	1 696	1 238	744	599	2 197	1 827
80-84	1 160	960	370	479	2 836	2 861	1 633	1 465	1 530	1 439
85+	958	830	304	339	...	...	...	...	1 262	1 169
Not stated غير محدد	650	673	1 269	1 054	...	...	...	...	1 919	1 727
Total المجموع	417 917	407 578	2 388 235	892 697	2 328 906	1 055 933	477 235	244 353	2 806 152	1 300 275

TABLE 17. POPULATION OF YEMEN BY AGE GROUP, 2004 CENSUS
الجدول ١٧ - السكان في اليمن بحسب الفئة العمرية، تعداد ٢٠٠٤

Age group الفئة العمرية	Nationals مواطنين		Non-nationals غير مواطنين		Urban حضر		Rural ريف		Total الجموع	
	Men رجال	Women نساء	Men رجال	Women نساء	Men رجال	Women نساء	Men رجال	Women نساء	Men رجال	Women نساء
<1	266 634	252 069	917	980	...	...	...	...	267 551	253 049
1-4	1 229 273	1 179 511	4 474	4 289	...	...	...	...	1 233 747	1 183 800
5-9	1 563 176	1 483 616	3 996	3 776	...	...	...	...	1 567 172	1 487 392
10-14	1 509 907	1 351 926	3 571	3 359	...	...	...	...	1 513 478	1 355 285
15-19	1 260 787	1 207 570	4 126	3 667	...	...	...	...	1 264 913	1 211 237
20-24	960 318	920 894	5 681	4 768	...	...	...	...	965 999	925 662
25-29	725 065	736 659	4 571	4 778	...	...	...	...	729 636	741 437
30-34	483 419	475 573	4 078	3 907	...	...	...	...	487 497	479 480
35-39	426 646	473 942	3 875	3 318	...	...	...	...	430 521	477 260
40-44	351 163	370 483	3 607	2 558	...	...	...	...	354 770	373 041
45-49	280 817	299 556	2 794	1 543	...	...	...	...	283 611	301 099
50-54	252 682	242 859	2 055	1 231	...	...	...	...	254 737	244 090
55-59	148 959	136 710	1 147	650	...	...	...	...	150 106	137 360
60-64	169 675	153 587	731	626	...	...	...	...	170 406	154 213
65-69	96 225	86 221	335	300	...	...	...	...	96 560	86 521
70-74	113 862	104 159	279	319	...	...	...	...	114 141	104 478
75-79	50 835	43 008	105	121	...	...	...	...	50 940	43 129
80-84	51 510	48 091	74	134	...	...	...	...	51 584	48 225
85+	42 151	36 399	99	132	...	...	...	...	42 250	36 531
Not stated غير محدد	6 677	4 676	657	243	...	...	...	...	7 334	4 919
Total الجموع	9 989 781	9 607 509	47 172	40 699	...	...	...	...	10 036 953	9 648 208

-28-

الفصل الثاني
Part II

التخصوبة والوفيات
Fertility and Mortality

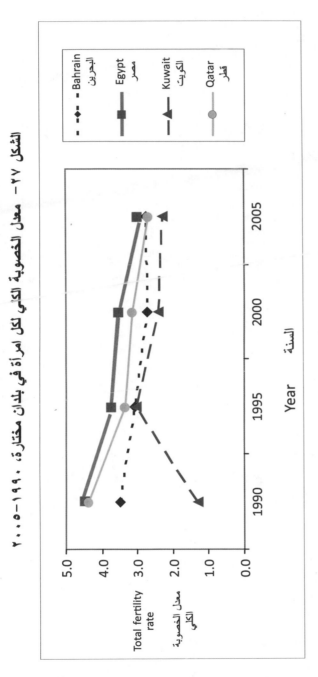

Figure 27. Total fertility rate per woman in selected countries, 1990-2005

الشكل - ٢٧ معدل الخصوبة الكلي لكل امرأة في بلدان مختارة، ١٩٩٠-٢٠٠٥

انخفض معدل الخصوبة الكلي في العراق بنسبة ٢,٤ في المائة فبلغ ٢,٦ طفل لكل امرأة، وهو أكبر انخفاض سجل في البلدان الأعضاء التي تتوفر عليها البيانات، وتليه الإمارات العربية المتحدة التي انخفض معدلها إلى النصف منذ عام ١٩٩٠ فبلغ ٢,٤ طفل. وانخفض معدل الخصوبة الكلي في مصر إلى ١، وفي قطر إلى ٢، وفي البحرين إلى ٣,١ و ٣,٠ على التوالي، وسجلت عُمان أول بياناتها في هذا المجال في عام ٢٠٠٧ حيث بلغ معدل الخصوبة الكلي ٢,٥. وسجلت عُمان أول بياناتها في هذا المجال في عام ٢٠٠٧ حيث بلغ معدل الخصوبة الكلي ٢,٥.

ومجلس التعاون الخليجي. فشهدت انخفاضات كبيرة منذ عام ١٩٩٠ في قطر (٧٢ في المائة)، والإمارات العربية المتحدة (٥٦ في المائة) والبحرين (٣٨ في المائة).

The total fertility rate in Iraq has fallen by 4.2 percentage points to 2.6 children per woman, the highest decrease in member countries with available data, followed by the United Arab Emirates, which has halved its rate to 2.4 since 1990. Egypt and Qatar have fallen to total fertility rates of 3.1 and 3.0 respectively and the rate in Bahrain has dropped to 2.8. In 2007, Oman recorded its first data point with a total fertility rate of 2.5.

The adolescent fertility rate has followed a similar trend, in particular in the GCC countries. Significant decreases have been seen in Qatar, the United Arab Emirates and Bahrain since 1990, representing falls of 72, 56 and 38 per cent respectively.

35

TABLE 18. LIVE BIRTHS, DEATHS, FOETAL, INFANT AND CHILD MORTALITY, AND MATERNAL DEATHS SINCE 1990

الجدول ١٨ – المواليد الأحياء والوفيات، ووفيات الأجنة والرضّع والأطفال، ووفيات الأمهات منذ عام ١٩٩٠

Country البلد	Year السنة	Live births المواليد الأحياء	Deaths الوفيات	Foetal deaths وفيات الأجنة	Infant deaths (0-1 yr) (صفر الى سنة) وفيات الرضّع	Child deaths (0-4 yrs) (صفر الى ٤ سنوات) وفيات الأطفال	Maternal deaths وفيات الأمهات
Bahrain البحرين	2007	16 062	2 270	...	133	165	3
	2006	15 053	2 317	...	115	152	2
	2005	15 198	2 222	...	134	165	1
	2004	14 968	2 215	...	135	161	3
	2003	14 560	2 114	...	107	138	3
	2002	13 576	2 035	...	94	121	3
	2001	13 468	1 979	...	117	162	3
	2000	13 947	2 045	...	117	154	2
	1995	13 481	1 910	...	254	285	6
	1990	13 370	1 553	...	272	296	2
Egypt مصر	2006	1 853 746	451 863	4 557	35 952	46 978	274
	2005	1 800 972	440 149	4 216	39 146	46 861	1 108
	2004	1 779 500	440 790	4 201	40 177	51 966	379
	2003	1 777 418	440 149	4 605	38 859	51 909	1 108
	2002	1 766 589	424 034	4 745	37 904	49 268	781
	2001	1 741 308	404 531	5 393	49 149	61 609	1 200
	2000	1 751 854	404 699	5 209	55 214	67 637	532
	1995	1 604 835	384 548	...	47 734	66 548	560
	1990	1 686 877	393 250	...	63 813	94 392	804
Iraq العراق	2005	896 340	115 775	...	12 460	...	...
	2004	840 257	101 820	...	10 972	...	...
	2003	691 269	95 935	...	9 638	...	...
	2002	746 771	85 758	...	12 447	...	...
	2001	716 861	77 727	...	...	...	...
	2000	471 886	179 928	...	...	81 804	...
	1995	455 727	138 784	...	...	55 823	...
	1990	660 385	32 464	...	14 998	8 903	...

36

TABLE 18 (*continued*)

الجدول ١٨ (تابع)

Country البلد	Year السنة	Live births المواليد الأحياء	Deaths الوفيات	Foetal deaths وفيات الأجنة	Infant deaths (0-1 yr) وفيات الرضّع (صفر إلى سنة)	Child deaths (0-4 yrs) وفيات الأطفال (صفر إلى ٤ سنوات)	Maternal deaths وفيات الأمهات
Jordan الأردن	2007	185 011	20 924	...	...	...	...
	2006	162 972	20 397	...	...	...	...
	2005	152 276	17 883	...	...	...	...
	2004	150 248	17 011	...	...	...	...
	2003	148 294	16 937	...	...	...	...
	2002	146 077	17 220	...	...	...	...
	2001	142 956	16 164	...	...	...	...
	2000	126 016	13 339	...	...	...	...
	1995	141 319	13 018	...	...	...	...
	1990	110 697	9 913	...	...	...	...
Kuwait الكويت	2007	53 587	5 293	374	449	533	1
	2006	52 759	5 247	347	456	533	1
	2005	50 941	4 784	375	420	504	2
	2004	47 274	4 793	355	422	510	6
	2003	43 982	4 424	307	412	497	4
	2002	43 490	4 342	325	418	492	3
	2001	41 342	4 364	286	420	507	1
	2000	41 843	4 227	269	379	492	4
	1995	40 790	3 781	...	450	529	3
	1990	...	...	...	...	...	...
Lebanon لبنان	2007	80 896	21 092	...	...	...	...
	2006	72 790	18 787	...	...	...	...
	2005	73 973	18 012	...	...	...	...
	2004	73 900	17 774	...	...	...	...
	2003	71 702	17 187	...	...	...	...
	2002	76 405	17 294	...	...	...	...
	2001	83 693	17 568	...	...	...	...

TABLE 18 (*continued*)

الجدول ١٨ (تابع)

Country	Year السنة	Live births المواليد الأحياء	Deaths الوفيات	Foetal deaths وفيات الأجنة	Infant deaths (0-1 yr) وفيات الرضع (صفر إلى سنة)	Child deaths (0-4 yrs) وفيات الأطفال (صفر إلى ٤ سنوات)	Maternal deaths وفيات الأمهات	البلد
	2000	87 795	19 435	...	...	...	...	
	1995	91 196	19 230	...	...	...	...	
	1990	70 903	13 263	...	...	...	...	
Oman[a/]	2007	48 041	6 449	449	423	51	2	عُمان[(١)]
	2006	44 116	5 814	367	381	57	3	
	2005	42 065	2 849	387	315	63	6	
	2004	40 584	2 743	346	336	55	3	
	2003	40 062	2 701	381	335	51	2	
	2002	40 222	2 564	376	332	71	7	
	2001	39 297	2 550	365	335	57	2	
	2000	39 994	2 547	388	369	59	2	
	1995	57 859	2 164	376	457	60	...	
	1990	51 943	2 090	573	681	61	...	
Palestine	2007	108 674	9 887	...	595	1 074	...	فلسطين
	2006	108 874	9 938	...	906	1 249	6	
	2005	109 439	9 645	...	1 057	1 384	1	
	2004	111 245	10 029	...	1 103	1 433	3	
	2003	106 355	10 207	...	1 150	1 542	7	
	2002	106 511	10 316	...	1 126	1 453	4	
	2001	103 780	9 177	...	1 138	1 504	5	
	2000	104 646	9 041	...	1 056	1 407	5	
	1995	104 470	8 398	...	1 654	2 096	...	
	1990	83 165	...	...	...	...	...	
Qatar	2007	15 681	1 776	95	117	142	5	قطر
	2006	14 120	1 750	79	114	151	1	
	2005	13 401	1 545	97	110	140	3	
	2004	13 190	1 341	64	113	137	1	
	2003	12 856	1 311	81	127	160	3	

TABLE 18 (*continued*)
الجدول ١٨ (تابع)

Country البلد	Year السنة	Live births المواليد الأحياء	Deaths الوفيات	Foetal deaths وفيات الأجنة	Infant deaths (0-1 yr) وفيات الرضيع (صفر إلى سنة)	Child deaths (0-4 yrs) وفيات الأطفال (صفر إلى ٤ سنوات)	Maternal deaths وفيات الأمهات
	2002	12 200	1 220	62	107	124	0
	2001	12 118	1 210	75	111	137	1
	2000	11 250	1 173	76	132	147	0
	1995	10 371	1 000	...	111	137	0
	1990	11 022	871	...	142	184	0
Saudi Arabia المملكة العربية السعودية							
	2007	595 099	95 166	...	10 782	12 571	...
	2006	589 223	93 752	...	10 954	12 796	...
	2005	582 582	92 487	...	11 078	12 974	...
	2004	574 211	91 243	...	11 164	13 099	...
	2003	567 433	89 976	...	11 224	13 283	...
	2002	560 746	92 486	...	11 299	13 470	...
	2001	554 147	91 319	...	11 377	13 662	...
	2000	547 637	86 291	...	11 489	13 857	...
	1995	552 778	75 430	...	13 468	15 900	...
	1990	364 686	22 396	...	8 436	10 031	...
Sudan السودان							
	2005	283 576	...	...	...	...	...
	2004	376 158	...	...	...	...	...
	2003	150 218	...	...	...	...	...
	2002	...	...	...	...	...	...
	2001	...	...	...	...	...	...
	2000	...	...	...	...	...	...
	1995	...	...	...	...	...	...
	1990	...	...	...	...	...	...
Syrian Arab Republic[b] الجمهورية العربية السورية[b]							
	2007	727 439	76 064	...	...	...	...
	2006	656 599	72 534	...	...	...	...
	2005	634 170	73 928	...	...	...	...
	2004	598 221	68 551	...	...	...	...

TABLE 18 (continued)
الجدول ١٨ (تابع)

Country البلد	Year السنة	Live births المواليد الأحياء	Deaths الوفيات	Foetal deaths وفيات الأجنة	Infant deaths (0-1 yr) وفيات الرضّع (صفر إلى سنة)	Child deaths (0-4 yrs) وفيات الأطفال (صفر إلى ٤ سنوات)	Maternal deaths وفيات الأمهات
	2003	609 774	62 880	...	...	...	...
	2002	574 918	62 184	...	...	...	...
	2001	524 212	60 814	...	...	...	...
	2000	505 484	57 759	...	...	...	...
	1995	478 308	52 214	...	...	...	...
	1990	414 667	46 946	...	...	...	...
United Arab Emirates الإمارات العربية المتحدة	2007	67 689	...	...	...	...	...
	2006	62 969	...	...	447	...	...
	2005	64 623	6 361	...	500	638	...
	2004	63 113	6 123	...	550	...	...
	2003	61 165	6 002	...	477	...	...
	2002	58 070	5 994	...	472	616	...
	2001	56 136	5 777	...	499	605	...
	2000	53 686	5 396	...	443	580	...
	1995	48 567	4 779	...	467	647	12
	1990	52 264	3 942	...	556	742	...
Yemen اليمن	2006 c/	275 716	20 607	...	...	...	...
	2005 c/	152 792	19 653	...	...	...	...
	2004	153 945	22 235	...	...	...	...
	2003	130 112	20 559	...	...	...	...
	2002	189 341	21 162	...	...	...	...
	2001	260 106	19 868	...	...	...	...
	2000	252 895	18 441	...	...	...	...
	1995	95 354	5 683	...	...	...	...
	1990	577 781	...	...	...	...	...

a/ Data for Omani nationals only. (أ) تشمل البيانات المواطنين العمانيين فقط.
b/ Data for Syrian nationals only. (ب) تشمل البيانات المواطنين السوريين فقط.
c/ Data on deaths refer only to Yemeni nationals. (ج) تشمل بيانات الوفيات المواطنين اليمنيين فقط.

TABLE 19. CRUDE BIRTH RATE; CRUDE DEATH RATE; RATE OF NATURAL INCREASE; FOETAL, INFANT AND CHILD MORTALITY RATES; AND MATERNAL MORTALITY RATIOS SINCE 1990[*]

الجدول ١٩ – معدل المواليد الخام، ومعدل الوفيات الخام، ومعدل الزيادة الطبيعية، ومعدلات وفيات الأجنة والرضّع والأطفال، ونسبة وفيات الأمهات منذ عام ١٩٩٠ (*)

Country البلد	Year السنة	Crude birth rate (per thousand) معدل المواليد الخام (في الألف)	Crude death rate (per thousand) معدل الوفيات الخام (في الألف)	Rate of natural increase (per cent) معدل الزيادة الطبيعية (في المائة)	Foetal mortality rate (per thousand) معدل وفيات الأجنة (في الألف)	Infant mortality rate (per thousand) معدل وفيات الرضّع (في الألف)	Child mortality rate (per thousand) معدل وفيات الأطفال (في الألف)	Maternal mortality ratio (per 100,000 live births) نسبة وفيات الأمهات (لكل مائة ألف ولادة حية)
Bahrain البحرين	2007	21.3	3.0	1.8	...	8.3	10.3	18.7
	2006	20.4	3.1	1.7	...	7.6	10.1	13.3
	2005	21.0	3.1	1.8	...	8.8	10.9	6.6
	2004	21.1	3.1	1.8	...	9.0	10.8	20.0
	2003	20.9	3.0	1.8	...	7.3	9.5	20.6
	2002	20.0	3.0	1.7	...	6.9	8.9	22.1
	2001	20.3	3.0	1.7	...	8.7	12.0	22.3
	2000	21.5	3.1	1.8	...	8.4	11.0	14.3
	1995	23.3	3.3	2.0	...	18.8	21.1	44.5
	1990	27.1	3.2	2.4	...	20.3	22.1	15.0
Egypt مصر	2006	25.0	6.1	1.9	2.5	19.4	25.3	14.8
	2005	24.7	6.0	1.9	2.3	21.7	26.0	61.5
	2004	24.9	6.2	1.9	2.4	22.6	29.2	21.3
	2003	25.3	6.3	1.9	2.6	21.9	29.2	62.3
	2002	25.6	6.1	1.9	2.7	21.5	27.9	44.2
	2001	25.7	6.0	2.0	3.1	28.2	35.4	68.9
	2000	26.3	6.1	2.0	3.0	31.5	38.6	30.4
	1995	26.5	6.3	2.0	...	29.7	41.5	34.9
	1990	30.6	7.1	2.3	...	37.8	56.0	47.7
Iraq العراق	2005	32.0	4.1	2.8	...	13.9	...	...
	2004	30.6	3.7	2.7	...	13.1	...	...
	2003	25.7	3.6	2.2	...	13.9	...	...

TABLE 19 (*continued*)

الجدول ١٩ (تابع)

Country	Year السنة	Crude birth rate (per thousand) معدل المواليد الخام (في الألف)	Crude death rate (per thousand) معدل الوفيات الخام (في الألف)	Rate of natural increase (per cent) معدل الزيادة الطبيعية (في المائة)	Foetal mortality rate (per thousand) معدل وفيات الأجنة (في الألف)	Infant mortality rate (per thousand) معدل وفيات الرضيع (في الألف)	Child mortality rate (per thousand) معدل وفيات الأطفال (في الألف)	Maternal mortality ratio (per 100,000 live births) نسبة وفيات الأمهات (لكل مائة ألف ولادة حية)	البلد
	2002	28.4	3.3	2.5	...	16.7	...	...	البلد
	2001	27.9	3.0	2.5	...	...	...	...	
	2000	18.8	7.2	1.2	...	...	173.4	...	
	1995	21.1	6.4	1.5	...	...	122.5	...	
	1990	35.7	1.8	3.4	...	22.7	13.5	...	
Jordan	2007	31.2	3.5	2.8	...	...	...	...	الأردن
	2006	28.4	3.6	2.5	...	...	...	...	
	2005	27.5	3.2	2.4	...	...	...	...	
	2004	28.0	3.2	2.5	...	...	...	...	
	2003	28.5	3.3	2.5	...	...	...	...	
	2002	28.9	3.4	2.5	...	...	...	...	
	2001	29.1	3.3	2.6	...	...	...	...	
	2000	26.3	2.8	2.3	...	...	...	...	
	1995	32.8	3.0	3.0	...	...	...	...	
	1990	34.0	3.0	3.1	...	...	...	...	
Kuwait	2007	18.8	1.9	1.7	7.0	8.4	9.9	1.9	الكويت
	2006	19.0	1.9	1.7	6.6	8.6	10.1	1.9	
	2005	18.9	1.8	1.7	7.4	8.2	9.9	3.9	
	2004	18.1	1.8	1.6	7.5	8.9	10.8	12.7	
	2003	17.4	1.7	1.6	7.0	9.4	11.3	9.1	
	2002	17.8	1.8	1.6	7.5	9.6	11.3	6.9	
	2001	17.7	1.9	1.6	6.9	10.2	12.3	2.4	
	2000	18.8	1.9	1.7	6.4	9.1	11.8	9.6	
	1995	23.6	2.2	2.1	...	11.0	13.0	7.4	
	1990	...	...	...	...	...	...	...	

TABLE 19 (continued)

الجدول ١٩ (تابع)

Country البلد	Year السنة	Crude birth rate (per thousand) معدل المواليد الخام (في الألف)	Crude death rate (per thousand) معدل الوفيات الخام (في الألف)	Rate of natural increase (per cent) معدل الزيادة الطبيعية (في المائة)	Foetal mortality rate (per thousand) معدل وفيات الأجنة (في الألف)	Infant mortality rate (per thousand) معدل وفيات الرضيع (في الألف)	Child mortality rate (per thousand) معدل وفيات الأطفال (في الألف)	Maternal mortality ratio (per 100,000 live births) نسبة وفيات الأمهات (لكل مائة ألف ولادة حية)
Lebanon لبنان	2007	19.7	5.1	1.5	...	...	...	...
	2006	17.9	4.6	1.3	...	...	...	...
	2005	18.4	4.5	1.4	...	...	...	...
	2004	18.6	4.5	1.4	...	...	...	...
	2003	18.3	4.4	1.4	...	...	...	...
	2002	19.7	4.5	1.5	...	...	...	...
	2001	21.9	4.6	1.7	...	...	...	...
	2000	23.3	5.2	1.8	...	...	...	...
	1995	26.1	5.5	2.1	...	...	...	...
	1990	23.8	4.5	1.9	...	...	...	...
Oman[a] عُمان	2007	18.5	2.5	1.6	9.3	8.8	1.1	22.9
	2006	17.3	2.3	1.5	8.3	8.6	1.3	13.2
	2005	16.8	1.1	1.6	9.2	7.5	1.5	15.4
	2004	16.4	1.1	1.5	8.5	8.3	1.4	18.5
	2003	16.3	1.1	1.5	9.5	8.4	1.3	23.2
	2002	16.5	1.0	1.5	9.3	8.3	1.8	37.5
	2001	16.2	1.1	1.5	9.3	8.5	1.5	23.1
	2000	16.6	1.1	1.6	9.7	9.2	1.5	16.1
	1995	26.6	1.0	2.6	6.5	7.9	1.0	...
	1990	28.2	1.1	2.7	11.0	13.1	1.2	...
Palestine فلسطين	2007	27.1	2.5	2.5	...	5.5	9.9	...
	2006	28.0	2.6	2.5	...	8.3	11.5	5.5
	2005	29.1	2.6	2.7	...	9.7	12.6	0.9
	2004	30.6	2.8	2.8	...	9.9	12.9	2.7

TABLE 19 (continued)
الجدول ١٩ (تابع)

Country البلد	Year السنة	Crude birth rate (per thousand) معدل المواليد الخام (في الألف)	Crude death rate (per thousand) معدل الوفيات الخام (في الألف)	Rate of natural increase (per cent) معدل الزيادة الطبيعية (في المائة)	Foetal mortality rate (per thousand) معدل وفيات الأجنة (في الألف)	Infant mortality rate (per thousand) معدل وفيات الرضيع (في الألف)	Child mortality rate (per thousand) معدل وفيات الأطفال (في الألف)	Maternal mortality ratio (per 100,000 live births) نسبة وفيات الأمهات (لكل مائة ألف ولادة حية)
	2003	30.3	2.9	2.7	...	10.8	14.5	6.6
	2002	31.4	3.0	2.8	...	10.6	13.6	3.8
	2001	31.8	2.8	2.9	...	11.0	14.5	4.8
	2000	33.2	2.9	3.0	...	10.1	13.4	4.8
	1995	39.9	3.2	3.7	...	15.8	20.1	...
	1990	38.6	...	...	...	...	...	...
Qatar قطر	2007	18.7	2.1	1.7	6.1	7.5	9.1	31.9
	2006	17.2	2.1	1.5	5.6	8.1	10.7	7.1
	2005	16.8	1.9	1.5	7.2	8.2	10.4	22.4
	2004	17.3	1.8	1.6	4.9	8.6	10.4	7.6
	2003	17.7	1.8	1.6	6.3	9.9	12.4	23.3
	2002	17.8	1.8	1.6	5.1	8.8	10.2	0.0
	2001	18.7	1.9	1.7	6.2	9.2	11.3	8.3
	2000	18.2	1.9	1.6	6.8	11.7	13.1	0.0
	1995	19.7	1.9	1.8	...	10.7	13.2	0.0
	1990	23.6	1.9	2.2	...	12.9	16.7	0.0
Saudi Arabia المملكة العربية السعودية	2007	24.1	3.8	2.0	...	18.1	21.1	...
	2006	24.4	3.9	2.0	...	18.6	21.7	...
	2005	24.7	3.9	2.1	...	19.0	22.3	...
	2004	24.9	4.0	2.1	...	19.4	22.8	...
	2003	25.2	4.0	2.1	...	19.8	23.4	...
	2002	25.6	4.2	2.1	...	20.1	24.0	...
	2001	25.9	4.3	2.2	...	20.5	24.7	...
	2000	26.3	4.1	2.2	...	21.0	25.3	...

TABLE 19 (*continued*)

الجدول ١٩ (تابع)

Country البلد	Year السنة	Crude birth rate (per thousand) معدل المواليد الخام (في الألف)	Crude death rate (per thousand) معدل الوفيات الخام (في الألف)	Rate of natural increase (per cent) معدل الزيادة الطبيعية (في المائة)	Foetal mortality rate (per thousand) معدل وفيات الأجنة (في الألف)	Infant mortality rate (per thousand) معدل وفيات الرضع (في الألف)	Child mortality rate (per thousand) معدل وفيات الأطفال (في الألف)	Maternal mortality ratio (per 100,000 live births) نسبة وفيات الأمهات (لكل مائة ألف ولادة حية)
Sudan السودان	1995	30.3	4.1	2.6	...	24.4	28.8	...
	1990	22.4	1.4	2.1	...	23.1	27.5	...
	2005	7.7	...	...	...	...	...	...
	2004	10.4	...	...	...	...	...	...
	2003	4.2	...	...	...	...	...	...
	2002	...	...	...	...	...	...	...
	2001	...	...	...	...	...	...	...
	2000	...	...	...	...	...	...	...
	1995	...	...	...	...	...	...	...
	1990	...	...	...	...	...	...	...
Syrian Arab Republic[b] الجمهورية العربية السورية(ب)	2007	36.5	3.8	3.3	...	...	...	...
	2006	33.8	3.7	3.0	...	...	...	...
	2005	33.6	3.9	3.0	...	...	...	...
	2004	32.5	3.7	2.9	...	...	...	...
	2003	34.1	3.5	3.1	...	...	...	...
	2002	33.0	3.6	2.9	...	...	...	...
	2001	30.9	3.6	2.7	...	...	...	...
	2000	30.6	3.5	2.7	...	...	...	...
	1995	...	...	...	...	...	...	...
	1990	...	...	...	...	...	...	...
United Arab Emirates الإمارات العربية المتحدة	2006	14.8	...	...	...	7.1	...	...
	2005	15.7	1.5	1.4	...	7.7	9.9	...

TABLE 19 (continued)
الجدول ١٩ (تابع)

Country البلد	Year السنة	Crude birth rate (per thousand) معدل الخام المواليد (في الألف)	Crude death rate (per thousand) معدل الوفيات الخام (في الألف)	Rate of natural increase (per cent) معدل الزيادة الطبيعية (في المائة)	Foetal mortality rate (per thousand) معدل وفيات الأجنة (في الألف)	Infant mortality rate (per thousand) معدل وفيات الرضع (في الألف)	Child mortality rate (per thousand) معدل وفيات الأطفال (في الألف)	Maternal mortality ratio (per 100,000 live births) نسبة وفيات الأمهات (لكل مائة ألف ولادة حية)
	2004	16.0	1.6	1.4	...	8.7	...	...
	2003	16.2	1.6	1.5	...	7.8	...	...
	2002	16.1	1.7	1.4	...	8.1	10.6	...
	2001	16.4	1.7	1.5	...	8.9	10.8	...
	2000	16.5	1.7	1.5	...	8.3	10.8	...
	1995	20.0	2.0	1.8	...	9.6	13.3	24.7
	1990	28.0	2.1	2.6	...	10.6	14.2	...
Yemen اليمن	2006 c/	12.7	0.9	1.2	...	...	...	...
	2005 c/	7.2	0.9	0.6	...	...	...	...
	2004	7.5	1.1	0.6	...	...	...	...
	2003	6.5	1.0	0.6	...	...	...	...
	2002	9.8	1.1	0.9	...	...	...	...
	2001	13.9	1.1	1.3	...	...	...	...
	2000	13.9	1.0	1.3	...	...	...	...
	1995	6.1	0.4	0.6	...	...	...	...
	1990	46.9	...	...	...	...	...	...

* Calculations are made on the basis of population estimates taken from United Nations *World Population Prospects: The 2006 Revision*.

a/ Data for Omani nationals only.

b/ Data for Syrian nationals only.

c/ Data on deaths refer only to Yemeni nationals.

(٢) احتسبت المعدلات استناداً إلى تقديرات السكان الواردة في منشور الأمم المتحدة "التوقعات السكانية في العالم: تنقيح عام ٢٠٠٦".

(*) تشمل بيانات الوفيات المواطنين العمانيين فقط.

(ب) تشمل البيانات المواطنين السوريين فقط.

(ج) تشمل بيانات الوفيات المواطنين اليمنيين فقط.

-46-

TABLE 20. GENERAL FERTILITY RATE; TOTAL FERTILITY RATE; ADOLESCENT FERTILITY RATE; GROSS REPRODUCTION RATE;
AND MEAN AGE AT CHILDBEARING SINCE 1990[*]

الجدول ٢٠ - معدل الخصوبة العام، ومعدل الخصوبة الكلي، ومعدل خصوبة المراهقات، ومعدل الإحلال الإجمالي،
ومتوسط عمر المرأة عند الإنجاب منذ عام ١٩٩٠ (*)

Country / السنة	Year / السنة	Female population (15-49 yrs) السكان النساء (١٥-٤٩ سنة)	Live births المواليد الأحياء	Female births المواليد الإناث	General fertility rate معدل الخصوبة العام	Total fertility rate (per woman) معدل الخصوبة الكلي (لكل امرأة)	Adolescent fertility rate (15-19 yrs) (per thousand) معدل خصوبة المراهقات (١٥-١٩) سنة (في الألف)	Gross reproduction rate (per woman) معدل الإحلال الإجمالي (لكل امرأة)	Mean age at childbearing متوسط عمر المرأة عند الإنجاب
Bahrain البحرين									
	2007	189 454	16 062	7 877	84.8	2.8	15.0	1.4	29.6
	2006	185 716	15 053	7 406	81.1	2.7	15.3	1.3	29.5
	2005	181 948	15 198	7 430	83.5	2.7	18.0	1.3	29.4
	2004	178 211	14 968	7 469	84.0	2.7	19.9	1.4	29.5
	2003	174 468	14 560	7 256	83.5	2.7	20.1	1.3	29.6
	2002	170 581	13 576	6 623	79.6	2.5	13.4	1.2	30.3
	2001	166 357	13 468	6 536	81.0	2.6	12.1	1.2	30.3
	2000	161 679	13 947	6 841	86.3	2.7	14.1	1.3	30.5
	1995	134 233	13 481	6 545	100.4	3.1	19.6	1.5	30.2
	1990	113 319	13 370	6 526	118.0	3.5	24.2	1.7	30.7
Egypt مصر									
	2006	19 232 828	1 853 746	902 661	96.4	3.1	26.2	1.5	28.8
	2005	18 861 206	1 800 972	881 835	95.5	3.1	23.7	1.5	28.6
	2004	13 468 637	1 779 500	877 341	96.4	3.2	22.9	1.6	28.9
	2003	18 057 524	1 777 418	877 320	98.4	3.3	22.8	1.6	29.0
	2002	17 633 828	1 766 591	861 038	100.2	3.3	18.9	1.6	29.0
	2001	17 206 286	1 741 308	846 358	101.2	3.4	18.6	1.6	28.8
	2000	16 781 546	1 751 854	847 098	104.4	3.5	17.0	1.7	29.0
	1995	14 720 117	1 604 835	769 150	109.0	3.7	13.2	1.8	29.6
	1990	12 765 262	1 686 877	815 564	132.1	4.4	13.6	2.2	30.4

TABLE 20 (continued)
الجدول ٢٠ (تابع)

Country الدلد	Year السنة	Female population (15-49 yrs) السكان النساء (15-49 سنة)	Live births المواليد الأحياء	Female births المواليد الإناث	General fertility rate معدل الخصوبة العام	Total fertility rate (per woman) معدل الخصوبة الكلي (لكل امرأة)	Adolescent fertility rate (15-19 yrs) (per thousand) معدل خصوبة المراهقات (15-19 سنة) (في الألف)	Gross reproduction rate (per woman) معدل الإحلال الإجمالي (لكل امرأة)	Mean age at childbearing متوسط عمر المرأة عند الإنجاب
Iraq العراق	2000	5 942 561	471 886	216 348	79.4	2.6	16.4	1.2	30.4
	1995	5 003 707	455 727	224 347	91.1	3.0	27.6	1.5	30.7
	1990	4 186 568	670 385	329 978	160.1	6.8	0.5	3.3	35.8
Kuwait الكويت	2007	712 101	53 587	26 129	75.3	2.3	13.2	1.1	29.5
	2006	692 312	52 759	25 836	76.2	2.3	14.3	1.1	29.6
	2005	669 739	50 941	25 019	76.1	2.3	14.2	1.1	29.7
	2004	644 616	47 274	23 039	73.3	2.2	15.2	1.1	29.6
	2003	617 499	43 982	21 569	71.2	2.2	16.3	1.1	29.5
	2002	588 647	43 490	21 356	73.9	2.2	16.3	1.1	29.5
	2001	558 415	41 342	20 316	74.0	2.2	17.5	1.1	29.4
	2000	527 414	41 843	20 511	79.3	2.4	17.3	1.2	29.6
	1995	402 253	41 169	20 216	102.3	3.0	32.7	1.5	29.4
	1991	449 731	20 609	10 013	45.8	1.3	10.5	0.6	29.0
Oman عمان	2007	584 020	48 041	23 585	82.3	2.5	7.6	1.3	30.2
Qatar قطر	2007	167 264	15 681	7 625	93.8	3.0	15.4	1.5	29.8
	2006	162 859	14 120	6 924	86.7	2.8	16.0	1.3	29.8
	2005	157 666	13 401	6 562	85.0	2.7	15.3	1.3	29.8
	2004	151 575	13 190	6 388	87.0	2.8	17.2	1.3	29.7
	2003	144 742	12 856	6 292	88.8	2.9	16.8	1.4	29.6
	2002	137 563	12 200	5 939	88.7	2.9	19.5	1.4	29.5
	2001	130 583	12 118	5 932	92.8	3.2	17.1	1.5	29.7

TABLE 20 (continued)

الجدول ٢٠ (تابع)

Country البلد	Year السنة	Female population (15-49 yrs) السكان النساء (١٥-٤٩) سنة	Live births المواليد الأحياء	Female births المواليد الإناث	General fertility rate معدل الخصوبة العام	Total fertility rate (per woman) معدل الخصوبة الكلي (لكل امرأة)	Adolescent fertility rate (15-19 yrs) (per thousand) معدل خصوبة المراهقات (١٥-١٩) سنة (في الألف)	Gross reproduction rate (per woman) معدل الإحلال الإجمالي (لكل امرأة)	Mean age at childbearing متوسط عمر المرأة عند الإنجاب
	2000	124 205	11 250	5 512	90.6	3.1	17.2	1.5	29.6
	1995	100 712	10 371	5 099	103.0	3.3	28.8	1.6	28.9
	1990	81 540	11 022	5 392	135.2	4.4	55.3	2.1	28.3
United Arab Emirates الإمارات العربية المتحدة									
	2003	757 930	61 165	29 924	80.7	2.4	23.5	1.2	30.9
	2002	710 548	58 070	28 562	81.7	2.5	21.6	1.2	30.8
	2001	664 194	56 136	27 518	84.5	2.6	21.6	1.3	30.9
	2000	621 067	53 686	26 046	86.4	2.7	21.9	1.3	31.1
	1995	455 264	48 567	23 816	106.7	3.3	37.2	1.6	30.4
	1990	336 056	52 264	25 394	155.5	4.8	53.5	2.3	29.3

* Rates are calculated on the basis of registered live births and population data taken from
World Population Prospects: The 2006 Revision.

(*) احتسبت المعدلات استناداً إلى بيانات الولادات الحية المسجلة وبيانات السكان الواردة في
منشور الأمم المتحدة "التوقعات السكانية في العالم: تنقيح عام ٢٠٠٦".

TABLE 21. TOTAL DEATHS BY CAUSE: CRUDE RATES AND PERCENTAGES, 2000-2007

الجدول ٢١ - مجموع الوفيات بحسب السبب: المعدلات الخام والنسب المئوية، ٢٠٠٠-٢٠٠٧

Cause of death	Total deaths			Rate per 100,000 population			Percentage		
	Total	Men	Women	Total	Men	Women	Total	Men	Women
Certain infectious and parasitic diseases	12 220	6 613	5 607	13.9	14.6	13.1	2.5	2.5	2.6
Neoplasms	28 488	16 293	12 195	32.3	35.9	28.5	5.9	6.1	5.7
Endocrine, nutritional and metabolic diseases	17 898	8 777	9 121	20.3	19.3	21.3	3.7	3.3	4.3
Diseases of the blood and blood-forming organs and certain disorders involving the immune mechanism	1 137	549	588	1.3	1.2	1.4	0.2	0.2	0.3
Mental and behavioural disorders	766	384	382	0.9	0.8	0.9	0.2	0.1	0.2
Diseases of the nervous system	7 538	4 036	3 502	8.5	8.9	8.2	1.6	1.5	1.7
Diseases of the circulatory system	183 828	97508	86320	208.4	214.9	201.6	38.3	36.5	40.7
Diseases of the respiratory system	28 847	15 534	13 313	32.7	34.2	31.1	6.0	5.8	6.3
Diseases of the digestive system	40 965	26 062	14 903	46.5	57.4	34.8	8.5	9.8	7.0
Diseases of the genito-urinary system	15 722	9 231	6 491	17.8	20.3	15.2	3.3	3.5	3.1
Pregnancy, childbirth and the puerperium	293	0	293	0.3	0.0	0.7	0.1	0.0	0.1
Diseases of the skin and subcutaneous tissue	196	81	115	0.2	0.2	0.3	0.0	0.0	0.1
Diseases of the musculoskeletal system and connective tissue	3 536	1 654	1 882	4.0	3.6	4.4	0.7	0.6	0.9

ESCWA region — منطقة الإسكوا

Latest year available — أخر سنة متوفرة

-50-

TABLE 21 (continued)
الجدول ٢١ (تابع)

ESCWA region منطقة الإسكوا أخر سنة متوفرة	Total deaths مجموع الوفيات			Rate per 100,000 population المعدل لكل مائة ألف من السكان			Percentage النسبة المئوية		
Latest year available									
Cause of death سبب الوفاة	Total	Men	Women	Total	Men	Women	Total	Men	Women
Congenital malformations, deformations and chromosomal abnormalities التشوهات الخلقية والعاهات والتشرذ الكروموزي	6 753	3 588	3 165	7.7	7.9	7.4	1.4	1.3	1.5
Certain conditions originating in the perinatal period حالات معينة تنشأ حول موعد الولادة	7 358	4 250	3 108	8.3	9.4	7.3	1.5	1.6	1.5
Symptoms, signs and abnormal clinical and laboratory findings, not classified elsewhere أعراض وعلامات ونتائج سريرية ومخبرية غير سريرية غير معنفة	98 798	53 544	45 254	112.0	118.0	105.7	20.6	20.0	21.3
Injury, poisoning and certain other consequences of external causes الإصابات والتسمم وغيرها من الحالات الناتجة عن أسباب خارجية	1 005	870	135	1.1	1.9	0.3	0.2	0.3	0.1
Codes for special purposes حالات غير مشخصة	21 415	16 075	5 340	24.3	35.4	12.5	4.5	6.0	2.5
Diseases of the eye and adnexa أمراض العين وتوابعها	0	0	0	0.0	0.0	0.0	0.0	0.0	0.0
Diseases of the ear and mastoid process أمراض الأذن والعملية الخشائية	0	0	0	0.0	0.0	0.0	0.0	0.0	0.0
External causes of morbidity and mortality أسباب خارجية للمرض والوفاة	2 058	1 750	308	2.3	3.9	0.7	0.4	0.7	0.1
Factors influencing health status and contact with health services عوامل تؤثر على الوضع الصحي والاتصال بالخدمات	659	452	207	0.7	1.0	0.5	0.1	0.2	0.1
المجموع Total	479 480	267 251	212 229	543.7	589.0	495.7	100	100	100
حجم السكان Population size	88 191 195	45 373 053	42 818 142	100 000	100 000	100 000			

TABLE 22. TOTAL DEATHS BY CAUSE: CRUDE RATES AND PERCENTAGES, 1990-1999

الجدول ٢٢ - مجموع الوفيات بحسب السبب: المعدلات الخام والنسب المئوية، ١٩٩٠-١٩٩٩

Cause of death	Total deaths مجموع الوفيات			Rate per 100,000 population المعدل (لكل مائة ألف من السكان)			Percentage النسبة المئوية			سبب الوفاة
ESCWA region Earliest year available	Total مجموع	Men رجال	Women نساء	Total مجموع	Men رجال	Women نساء	Total مجموع	Men رجال	Women نساء	منطقة الإسكوا أول سنة متوفرة
Certain infectious and parasitic diseases	32 904	16 211	16 693	50.6	48.4	52.9	8.1	7.6	8.7	امراض معدية وطفيلية معينة
Neoplasms	13 888	8 153	5 735	21.4	24.4	18.2	3.4	3.8	3.0	الأورام
Endocrine, nutritional and metabolic diseases	10 503	4 702	5 801	16.2	14.1	18.4	2.6	2.2	3.0	امراض الغدد الصماء والتغذية
Diseases of the blood and blood-forming organs and certain disorders involving the immune mechanism	1 955	1 163	792	3.0	3.5	2.5	0.5	0.5	0.4	امراض الدم واعضاء تكوين الدم واضطرابات معينة تشمل اضطرابات المناعة
Mental and behavioural disorders	251	137	114	0.4	0.4	0.4	0.1	0.1	0.1	الاضطرابات العقلية والسلوكية
Diseases of the nervous system	6 539	3 674	2 865	10.1	11.0	9.1	1.6	1.7	1.5	امراض الجهاز العصبي
Diseases of the circulatory system	173 661	89 408	84 253	267.2	267.2	267.1	42.8	41.8	43.9	امراض جهاز الدورة الدموية
Diseases of the respiratory system	54 125	27 430	26 695	83.3	82.0	84.6	13.3	12.8	13.9	امراض الجهاز التنفسي
Diseases of the digestive system	19 733	11 885	7 848	30.4	35.5	24.9	4.9	5.6	4.1	امراض الجهاز الهضمي
Diseases of the genito-urinary system	16 618	10 013	6 605	25.6	29.9	20.9	4.1	4.7	3.4	امراض الجهاز التناسلي والبولي
Pregnancy, childbirth and the puerperium	816	4	812	1.3	0.0	2.6	0.2	0.0	0.4	مضاعفات الحمل والولادة والنفاس
Diseases of the skin and subcutaneous tissue	43	17	26	0.1	0.1	0.1	0.0	0.0	0.0	امراض الجلد والنسيج تحت الجلد
Diseases of the musculoskeletal system and connective tissue	166	77	89	0.3	0.2	0.3	0.0	0.0	0.0	امراض الجهاز العضلي والنسيج الضام والهيكل

TABLE 22 (continued)
الجدول ٢٢ (تابع)

ESCWA region / منطقة الإسكوا Earliest year available / أول سنة متوفرة Cause of death / سبب الوفاة	Total deaths مجموع الوفيات			Rate per 100,000 population المعدل (لكل مائة ألف من السكان)			Percentage النسبة المئوية		
	Total مجموع	Men رجال	Women نساء	Total مجموع	Men رجال	Women نساء	Total مجموع	Men رجال	Women نساء
Congenital malformations, deformations and chromosomal abnormalities / التشوهات والتشرذ الكروموزي الخلقية والتشوهات	4 620	2 387	2 233	7.1	7.1	7.1	1.1	1.1	1.2
Certain conditions originating in the perinatal period / حالات معينة تنشأ حول موعد الولادة	7 871	4 679	3 192	12.1	14.0	10.1	1.9	2.2	1.7
Symptoms, signs and abnormal clinical and laboratory findings, not classified elsewhere / أعراض وعلامات ونتائج سريرية ومخبرية غير معينة غير مصنفة	41 530	20 114	21 416	63.9	60.1	67.9	10.2	9.4	11.2
Injury, poisoning and certain other consequences of external causes / الإصابات والتسمم وغيرها من الحالات الناتجة عن أسباب خارجية	19 477	13 044	6 433	30.0	39.0	20.4	4.8	6.1	3.4
Codes for special purposes / حالات غير مشخصة	839	608	231	1.3	1.8	0.7	0.2	0.3	0.1
Total / المجموع	405 539	213 706	191 833	623.9	638.6	608.2	100	100	100
Population size / حجم السكان	65 003 951	33 463 166	31 540 785	100 000	100 000	100 000			

الفصل الثالث
Part III

الزواج والطلاق
Marriage and Divorce

In the ESCWA region, as in many others, marriage is seen as a social sanction required for a man and a woman to live together and enter into a legitimate sexual relationship for the biological continuity of the population. Marriage and its dissolution are important proximate determinants of fertility. Studying data on the age at first marriage enables its impact on fertility to be assessed, as early marriage has a greater impact on fertility than later marriage. In recent years, Arab countries have faced rapid changes in nuptiality patterns as a consequence of social changes. Such factors as increased numbers of women being employed outside the home, greater female autonomy and increased life expectancy for both sexes have had a considerable effect on the demographic process.

Fewer and later marriages in Lebanon; more and earlier marriages in Palestine

Mean age at first marriage in the ESCWA region has been increasing gradually over the past 17 years for both women and men. In Bahrain, the mean age for both sexes has increased for nationals and non-nationals: in 2006, the mean age at first marriage for women was 23.2 years, a rise from 22.3 years in 1990, while that for men was 27.6 years, an increase from 26.1 years in 1990. In Egypt, while the mean age at first marriage for women increased from 22.1 years in 1990 to 23.5 years in 2007, the mean age for men remained steady at around 28.5 years.

ينظر إلى الزواج في منطقة الإسكوا كما في مناطق أخرى، باعتباره شرعية اجتماعية مطلوبة لكي يعيش رجل وامرأة معا ويدخلان في علاقة جنسية شرعية من أجل ضمان الاستمرارية البيولوجية للسكان. ويعتبر الزواج وانهياره من المحددات المباشرة الهامة للخصوبة. ودراسة البيانات عن العمر لدى الزواج الأول تساعد على تقييم تأثير ذلك على الخصوبة، لأن الزواج المبكر له تأثير أكبر على الخصوبة من الزواج المتأخر. وشهدت البلدان العربية في السنوات الماضية تغيرات سريعة في أنماط الزواج نتيجة للتغيرات الاجتماعية. وكان لعوامل مثل زيادة عدد النساء العاملات خارج المنزل، وزيادة استقلالية الأنثى، وزيادة العمر المتوقع للرجل والنساء على السواء، تأثير كبير على العملية الديمغرافية.

زيجات أقل وأكثر تأخراً في لبنان وزيجات أكثر وأبكر في فلسطين

سجل ارتفاع تدريجي في متوسط العمر عند الزواج الأول للرجال والنساء في منطقة الإسكوا خلال الـ ١٧ سنة الماضية. وفي البحرين ارتفع متوسط العمر عند الزواج الأول للجنسين من المواطنين والأجانب، حيث ارتفع متوسط العمر عند الزواج الأول للنساء من ٢٢.٣ سنة في عام ١٩٩٠ إلى ٢٣.٢ سنة في عام ٢٠٠٦، وللرجال من ٢٦.١ سنة في عام ١٩٩٠ إلى ٢٧.٦ سنة في عام ٢٠٠٦. وفي مصر، سجل متوسط العمر عند الزواج الأول للنساء ارتفاعا من ٢٢.١ سنة في عام ١٩٩٠ إلى ٢٣.٥ سنة في عام ٢٠٠٧، بينما في متوسط العمر عند الزواج الأول للرجال في حدود ٢٨.٥ سنة.

وسُجّلت أكبر زيادة في متوسط العمر عند الزواج الأول في المنطقة في الأردن وعُمان. ففي الأردن، ارتفع متوسط العمر عند الزواج الأول للنساء من ٢١.٥ سنة في عام ١٩٩٠ إلى ٢٦.٣ سنة في عام ٢٠٠٧، بينما كانت الزيادة أقل للرجال من ٢٥.٩ سنة في عام ١٩٩٠ إلى ٢٩.٤ سنة في عام ٢٠٠٧. وكذلك في عُمان، حيث ارتفع متوسط العمر عند الزواج الأول للنساء من ٢٠.٣ سنة في عام ١٩٩٠ إلى ٢٥ سنة في عام ٢٠٠٣، وللرجال من ٢٣.٢ سنة في عام ١٩٩٠ إلى ٢٨ سنة في عام ٢٠٠٣. أما لبنان، فسجّل أعلى متوسط للعمر عند الزواج الأول من المنطقة، إذ بلغ هذا المتوسط للنساء ٢٨.٨ سنة وللرجال ٣٢.٨ سنة في عام ٢٠٠٤، وتليه الجمهورية العربية السورية حيث بلغ متوسط العمر عند الزواج الأول للنساء ٢٦.٨ سنة في عام ٢٠٠٦، بعد أن كان ٢٥.١ سنة في عام ٢٠٠٠، وللرجال ٣٠.٦ سنة في عام ٢٠٠٦ بعد أن كان ٢٨.٩ سنة في عام ٢٠٠٠.

ومع أن فلسطين وقطر والمملكة العربية السعودية شهدت تغيراً في متوسط العمر عند الزواج الأول للرجال والنساء على السواء، إلا أن التغيير لم يكن بحجم التغيير الذي شهدته بلدان أخرى. فأحدث البيانات المتوفرة عن فلسطين تفيد بأن متوسط العمر عند الزواج الأول بلغ ١٩.٤ سنة للنساء و ٢٤.٦ سنة للرجال. وعلى الرغم من أن معدلات فلسطين تُعتبر هي الأدنى لمتوسط العمر عند الزواج الأول في منطقة الإسكوا، إلا أنها تعكس زيادة من ١٨ سنة و ٢٣ سنة على التوالي في عام ١٩٩٠. وفي قطر، زاد متوسط العمر عند الزواج الأول للنساء من ٢٢.٩ سنة وللرجال ٢٦.١ سنة في عام ١٩٩٥ إلى ٢٣.٧ سنة و ٢٦.٥ سنة في عام ٢٠٠٧. وفي المملكة العربية السعودية، ارتفع متوسط العمر عند الزواج الأول للنساء من ٢١.٩ سنة وللرجال ٢٧.٢ سنة في عام ٢٠٠٤ إلى ٢٤.٦ سنة في عام ٢٠٠٧.

The largest increase in mean age at first marriage in the region was seen in Jordan and Oman. In Jordan, the mean age at first marriage for women increased from 21.5 years in 1990 to 26.3 years in 2007; the increase for men was slightly lower, from 25.9 years in 1990 to 29.4 years in 2007. Similarly, in Oman, the mean age at first marriage for women increased from 20.3 years in 1990 to 25.0 years in 2003, while that for men rose from 23.2 years in 1990 to 28.0 years in 2003. Lebanon, however, has the highest mean age at first marriage in the region: 28.8 years for women and 32.8 years for men in 2004, followed by the Syrian Arab Republic: 26.8 years for women in 2006, a rise from 25.1 years in 2000, and 30.6 years for men in 2006, an increase from 28.9 years in 2000.

In Palestine, Qatar and Saudi Arabia, while there has been a change in the mean age at first marriage for both women and men, the difference is less significant than in other countries. The latest available data for Palestine shows the mean age at first marriage is 19.4 years for women and 24.6 years for men; while these are the youngest mean ages at first marriage in the ESCWA region, they still represent an increase from 18 years and 23 years respectively in 1990. In Qatar, the mean age at first marriage increased from 22.9 years for women and 26.1 years for men in 1995 to 23.7 years and 26.5 years respectively in 2007. In Saudi Arabia, 2007 data shows the mean age at first marriage is 24.6 years for women and 27.2 years for men, compared with 24.1 years and 26.9 years respectively in 2004.

وارتفع معدل الزواج الخام في معظم البلدان الأعضاء في الإسكوا باستثناء كل من الكويت حيث سجل هذا المعدل انخفاضا طفيفا من ٥.٥ إلى ٤.٧ بين عامي ١٩٩٥ و٢٠٠٧ ولبنان حيث سجل تراجعا من ١٠.١ إلى ٨.٧ بين عامي ١٩٩٠ و٢٠٠٧. أما بالنسبة إلى البلدان الأخرى، فارتفع معدل الزواج الخام في البحرين من ٦.٠ إلى ٦.٤ في عام ٢٠٠٦، وفي مصر من ٧.٣ إلى ٨.١ في عام ٢٠٠٧. وفي العراق من ٧.٨ إلى ٩.٦ في عام ٢٠٠٤، وفي الأردن من ١٠.١ في عام ١٩٩٠ إلى ١٠.٢ في عام ٢٠٠٧. وتميزت الإمارات العربية المتحدة وقطر بأدنى معدلات للزواج في المنطقة بلغت ٣.٨ و٣.١ على التوالي في عام ٢٠٠٧ و٢٠٠٥، بينما تميزت فلسطين بأعلى معدل للزواج الخام بلغ ١٥.٢ في عام ١٩٩٠ وارتفع إلى ١٦.٣ في عام ٢٠٠٧.

وفي عام ٢٠٠٧ كان أكبر عدد للزيجات المسجلة في الأردن حيث بلغ ٦٠ ٥٤٨ زواجا، وشكل ارتفاعا نسبة ٨٥.١ في المائة مقارنة بعام ١٩٩٠. وتلاها العراق، حيث زاد عدد الزيجات المسجلة بنسبة ٨٢.٩ في المائة بين عامي ١٩٩٠ و٢٠٠٤ ثم البحرين، حيث بلغ عدد الزيجات المسجلة ٤ ٧٢٤ زواجا في عام ٢٠٠٦، أي بزيادة نسبتها ٦٠.٦ في المائة مقارنة بعام ١٩٩٠. وزاد عدد الزيجات المسجلة في مصر في عام ٢٠٠٧ بنسبة ٥١.٨ في المائة مقارنة بعام ١٩٩٠. وفي الكويت بنسبة ٣٩.٩ في المائة مقارنة بعام ١٩٩٠، بينما سجل لبنان أدنى زيادة في هذا المعدل حيث بلغ ٢٣ ٧٩٦ زواجا في عام ٢٠٠٧، أي بزيادة نسبتها ١٩.٥ في المائة فقط مقارنة بعام ١٩٩٠.

In 2007, the highest number of marriage registrations in the ESCWA region was in Jordan, where 60,548 marriages were registered, representing an increase of 85.1 per cent since 1990. Jordan was followed by Iraq, where the number of marriages registered increased by 82.9 per cent between 1990 and 2004, and Bahrain, where the 4,724 marriages registered in 2006 represented an increase of 60.6 per cent since 1990. The number of marriages registered in Egypt and Kuwait in 2007 increased by 51.8 per cent and 39.9 per cent respectively from 1990 figures, while Lebanon recorded the lowest increase, with 35,796 marriages registered in 2007, a rise of just 19.5 per cent since 1990.

The crude marriage rate has increased in most ESCWA member countries, although it has declined in Kuwait and Lebanon, falling slightly from 5.5 to 4.7 between 1995 and 2007 in Kuwait and from 10.1 to 8.7 between 1990 and 2007 in Lebanon. The crude marriage rate in Bahrain was 6.4 in 2006, an increase from 6.0 in 1990. In Egypt, it was 8.1 in 2007, an increase from 7.3 in 1990. Iraq and Jordan have also seen a rise in crude marriage rates: 9.6 in Iraq in 2004, compared with 7.8 in 1990, and 10.2 in Jordan in 2007, a slight increase from the 10.1 registered in 1990. The United Arab Emirates and Qatar have the lowest crude marriage rates within the region at 3.8 and 3.1 in 2007 and 2005 respectively, while Palestine has the highest rate: 16.3 in 2007, a rise from 15.2 in 1990.

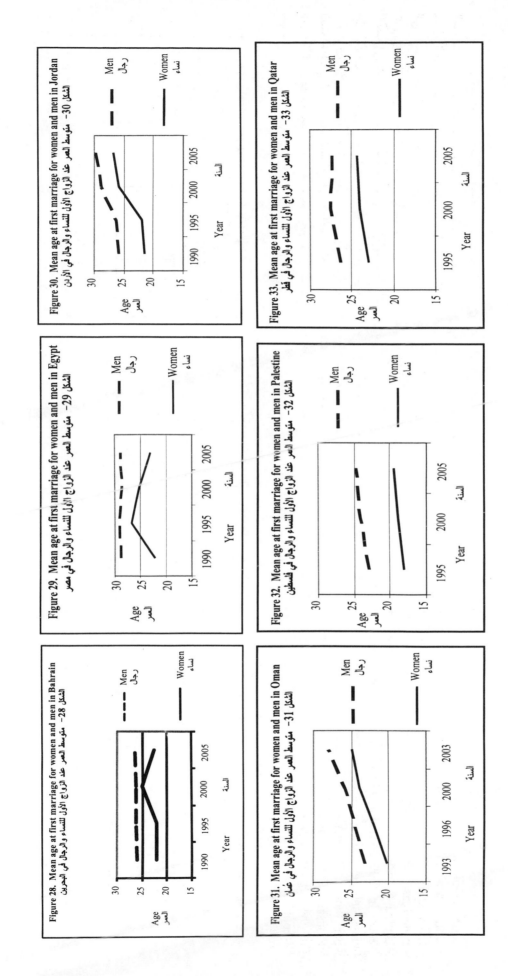

Figure 28. Mean age at first marriage for women and men in Bahrain الشكل 28- متوسط العمر عند الزواج الأول للنساء والرجال في البحرين

Men رجال

Women نساء

Figure 29. Mean age at first marriage for women and men in Egypt الشكل 29- متوسط العمر عند الزواج الأول للنساء والرجال في مصر

Men رجال

Women نساء

Figure 30. Mean age at first marriage for women and men in Jordan الشكل 30- متوسط العمر عند الزواج الأول للنساء والرجال في الأردن

Men رجال

Women نساء

Figure 31. Mean age at first marriage for women and men in Oman الشكل 31- متوسط العمر عند الزواج الأول للنساء والرجال في عمان

Men رجال

Women نساء

Figure 32. Mean age at first marriage for women and men in Palestine الشكل 32- متوسط العمر عند الزواج الأول للنساء والرجال في فلسطين

Men رجال

Women نساء

Figure 33. Mean age at first marriage for women and men in Qatar الشكل 33- متوسط العمر عند الزواج الأول للنساء والرجال في قطر

Men رجال

Women نساء

Despite a decline, Egypt still has the highest number of divorces

Latest available data show that the divorce rate in Saudi Arabia is little more than one third of that in Egypt. In 2007, Qatar registered 997 divorces, the lowest number in the region, yet representing the highest percentage increase (177.7 per cent) since 1990, followed by the Syrian Arab Republic, with a 133.8 per cent increase (19,506 divorces registered in 2007).

The crude divorce rate has increased in most ESCWA member countries in recent years. However, rates in Egypt, Palestine and the United Arab Emirates have declined. In Egypt, the crude divorce rate fell slightly from 1.2 in 1990 to 1.0 per thousand in 2007; in Palestine, it decreased from 2.3 in 2000 to 2.0 per thousand in 2007; and in the United Arab Emirates, it fell from 1.1 in 1990 to 0.8 per thousand in 2005. In 2007, Jordan and Palestine recorded the highest crude divorce rates in the region at 2.0 per thousand, followed by Kuwait (1.7 per thousand), Bahrain (1.5 per thousand) and Lebanon (1.5 per thousand). The United Arab Emirates had the lowest crude divorce rate in the region at 0.8 per thousand, followed by the Syrian Arab Republic, Saudi Arabia and Egypt (all at 1.0 per thousand).

ما زالت مصر تسجل أكبر عدد لحالات الطلاق رغم انخفاض هذا العدد

تفيد أحدث البيانات المتوفرة بأن معدل الطلاق في مصر يقابل ورغم أن قطر سجلت أدنى عدد من ثلث هذا المعدل في المملكة العربية السعودية. وفي عام 2007، سجلت قطر أدنى عدد من حالات الطلاق في المنطقة بالغ 997 طلاقاً في عام 2007، إلا أن هذا شكل أعلى نسبة ارتفاع منذ عام 1990 بلغت 177.7 في المائة، تليها الجمهورية العربية السورية حيث سجلت ارتفاع 133.8 في المائة (أي بزيادة بلغت نسبتها 19,506 حالة طلاق في عام 2007).

وارتفع معدل الطلاق الخام في معظم البلدان الأعضاء في الإسكوا. فقد سجلت السورات الأخيرة باستثناء مصر وفلسطين والإمارات العربية المتحدة. ففي مصر انخفض طفيفاً من 1.2 في عام 1990 إلى 1.0 في الألف في عام 2007، وفي فلسطين من 2.3 في عام 2000 إلى 2.0 في الألف في عام 2007، وفي الإمارات العربية المتحدة من 1.1 في عام 1990 إلى 0.8 في الألف في عام 2005. وسجلت أعلى المعدلات الطلاق الخام في عام 2007 في الأردن وفلسطين حيث بلغت 2 في الألف، يليهما الكويت (1.7 في الألف) والبحرين (1.5 في الألف) ولبنان (1.5 في الألف). وشهدت الإمارات العربية المتحدة أدنى معدل خام للطلاق في المنطقة بلغ 0.8 في الألف، تليها الجمهورية العربية السورية والمملكة العربية السعودية ومصر حيث سجل معدل 1 في الألف لكل منها.

الشكل 36. معدلات الزواج الخام في العراق
Figure 36. Crude marriage rates in Iraq

الشكل 35. معدلات الزواج والطلاق الخام في مصر
Figure 35. Crude marriage and divorce rates in Egypt

الشكل 34. معدلات الزواج والطلاق الخام في البحرين
Figure 34. Crude marriage and divorce rates in Bahrain

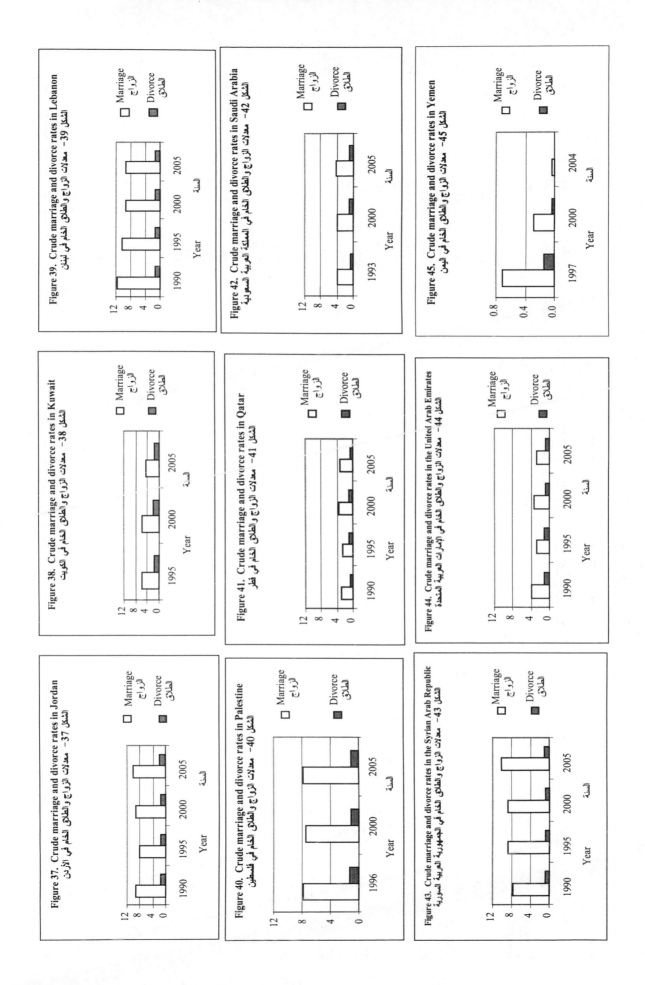

Figure 37. Crude marriage and divorce rates in Jordan
الشكل 37- معدلات الزواج والطلاق الخام في الأردن

Figure 38. Crude marriage and divorce rates in Kuwait
الشكل 38- معدلات الزواج والطلاق الخام في الكويت

Figure 39. Crude marriage and divorce rates in Lebanon
الشكل 39- معدلات الزواج والطلاق الخام في لبنان

Figure 40. Crude marriage and divorce rates in Palestine
الشكل 40- معدلات الزواج والطلاق الخام في فلسطين

Figure 41. Crude marriage and divorce rates in Qatar
الشكل 41- معدلات الزواج والطلاق الخام في قطر

Figure 42. Crude marriage and divorce rates in Saudi Arabia
الشكل 42- معدلات الزواج والطلاق الخام في المملكة العربية السعودية

Figure 43. Crude marriage and divorce rates in the Syrian Arab Republic
الشكل 43- معدلات الزواج والطلاق الخام في الجمهورية العربية السورية

Figure 44. Crude marriage and divorce rates in the United Arab Emirates
الشكل 44- معدلات الزواج والطلاق الخام في الإمارات العربية المتحدة

Figure 45. Crude marriage and divorce rates in Yemen
الشكل 45- معدلات الزواج والطلاق الخام في اليمن

TABLE 23. MEAN AGE AT FIRST MARRIAGE
الجدول ٢٣ - متوسط العمر عند الزواج الأول

Country / Year	Nationals مواطنون Men رجال	Women نساء	Non-nationals غير مواطنين Men رجال	Women نساء	Urban حضر Men رجال	Women نساء	Rural ريف Men رجال	Women نساء	Total المجموع Men رجال	Women نساء
Bahrain البحرين										
2007	...	...	...	24.8	...	...	...	...	...	23.2
2006	27.1	23.0	28.3	24.3	...	...	...	...	27.6	22.7
2005	26.2	22.5	27.7	24.9	...	...	...	...	26.5	22.8
2004	26.2	22.5	28.2	24.8	...	...	...	...	26.5	22.7
2003	26.5	22.5	27.2	25.9	...	...	...	...	26.6	22.8
2002	26.4	22.4	30.8	25.8	...	...	...	...	26.6	22.9
2001	26.5	22.5	28.0	25.4	...	...	...	...	26.6	25.0
2000	26.2	22.3	27.8	26.4	...	...	...	...	26.3	22.2
1995	26.1	21.8	28.1	25.4	...	...	...	...	26.3	22.3
1990	25.9	21.5	27.5	...	...	...	...	...	26.1	...
Egypt مصر										
2007*	...	...	...	...	...	...	...	...	28.5	23.5
2006	...	...	...	...	...	...	...	...	28.8	23.0
2005	...	...	...	...	...	...	...	...	28.8	23.2
2004	...	...	...	...	...	...	...	...	28.6	22.1
2003	...	...	...	...	...	...	...	...	29.0	23.1
2002	...	...	...	...	...	...	...	...	29.2	23.1
2001	...	...	...	...	...	...	...	...	28.7	25.5
2000	...	...	...	...	...	...	...	...	28.6	25.3
1995	...	...	...	...	...	...	...	...	29.0	26.7
1990	...	...	...	...	...	...	...	...	28.7	22.1
Jordan الأردن										
2007	...	...	...	...	29.5	26.2	29.1	26.8	29.4	26.3
2006	...	...	...	...	29.9	26.6	29.6	27.3	29.8	26.8
2005	...	...	...	...	...	...	...	...	29.7	26.8
2004	...	...	...	...	...	...	...	...	29.3	25.9
2003	...	...	...	...	...	...	...	...	29.8	27.2

TABLE 23 (continued)
الجدول ٢٣ (تابع)

Country البلد	Year السنة	Nationals مواطنون Men رجال	Women نساء	Non-nationals غير مواطنين Men رجال	Women نساء	Urban حضر Men رجال	Women نساء	Rural ريف Men رجال	Women نساء	Total المجموع Men رجال	Women نساء
	2002	...	...	...	...	...	...	...	...	29.3	26.8
	2001	...	...	...	...	...	...	...	...	29.3	26.6
	2000	...	...	...	...	...	...	...	...	28.9	25.9
	1995	...	...	...	...	...	...	...	...	26.4	21.9
	1990	...	...	...	...	...	...	...	...	25.9	21.5
Lebanon لبنان	2007	...	...	...	...	...	...	...	...	...	...
	2006	...	...	...	...	...	...	...	...	...	...
	2005	...	...	...	...	...	...	...	...	...	...
	2004	...	...	...	...	...	...	...	...	32.8	28.8
	2003	...	...	...	...	...	...	...	...	...	...
	2002	...	...	...	...	...	...	...	...	...	...
	2001	...	...	...	...	...	...	...	...	...	...
	2000	...	...	...	...	...	...	...	...	...	...
	1995	...	...	...	...	...	...	...	...	...	...
	1990	...	...	...	...	...	...	...	...	...	...
Oman غنان	2007	...	...	...	...	...	...	...	...	...	...
	2006	...	...	...	...	...	...	...	...	...	...
	2005	...	...	...	...	...	...	...	...	...	...
	2004	...	...	...	...	...	...	...	...	...	...
	2003	28.0	25.0	...	...	...	...	...	...	...	...
	2002	...	...	...	...	...	...	...	...	...	...
	2001	...	...	...	...	...	...	...	...	...	...
	2000	26.0	24.0	...	...	...	...	...	...	...	...
	1996	24.6	22.0	...	...	...	...	...	...	...	...
	1993	23.2	20.3	...	...	...	...	...	...	...	...

TABLE 23 *(continued)*

الجدول ٢٣ (تابع)

Country	Year	Nationals مواطنين		Non- nationals غير مواطنين		Urban حضر		Rural ريف		Total المجموع	
		Men رجال	Women نساء	Men رجال	Women نساء	Men رجال	Women نساء	Men رجال	Women نساء	Men رجال	Women نساء
Palestine فلسطين	2007	24.6	19.4	...	...	...	...	...	...	...	...
	2006	24.7	19.5	...	...	...	...	...	...	...	...
	2005	24.7	19.4	...	...	...	...	...	...	...	...
	2004	24.6	19.3	...	...	...	...	...	...	...	...
	2003	24.6	19.4	...	...	...	...	...	...	...	...
	2002	24.2	19.0	...	...	...	...	...	...	...	...
	2001	24.2	19.0	...	...	...	...	...	...	...	...
	2000	24.1	18.9	...	...	...	...	...	...	...	...
	1995	23.0	18.0	...	...	...	...	...	...	...	...
	1990	...	...	...	...	...	...	...	...	...	...
Qatar قطر	2007	26.5	23.7	29.0	27.4	...	...	...	...	27.5	24.6
	2006	26.4	23.6	28.9	25.6	...	...	...	...	27.3	24.3
	2005	26.7	23.9	28.8	25.1	...	...	...	...	27.4	24.3
	2004	29.2	24.8	28.9	24.5	...	...	...	...	28.9	24.7
	2003	27.3	24.1	29.4	24.4	...	...	...	...	27.8	24.5
	2002	27.1	23.8	28.9	24.9	...	...	...	...	27.6	24.1
	2001	27.0	23.8	28.8	25.1	...	...	...	...	27.4	24.2
	2000	27.1	23.8	28.7	24.7	...	...	...	...	27.5	24.0
	1995	26.1	22.9	26.9	23.3	...	...	...	...	26.3	23.0
	1990	...	...	...	...	...	...	...	...	...	...
Saudi Arabia المملكة العربية السعودية	2007	27.2	24.6	...	...	...	...	...	...	...	...
	2006	...	...	...	...	...	...	...	...	...	...
	2005	...	...	...	...	...	...	...	...	...	...
	2004	26.9	24.1	...	...	...	...	...	...	...	...
	2003	...	...	...	...	...	...	...	...	...	...

TABLE 23 (continued)
الجدول ٢٣ (تابع)

| Country | Year | Nationals | | Non-nationals | | Urban | | Rural | | Total | |
| المنطقة | السنة | مواطنين | | غير مواطنين | | حضر | | ريف | | المجموع | |
		Men رجال	Women نساء	Men رجال	Women نساء	Men رجال	Women نساء	Men رجال	Women نساء	Men رجال	Women نساء
	2002	..	..	..	..	..	..	..	..	..	..
	2001	..	..	..	..	..	..	..	..	..	..
	2000	..	..	..	..	..	..	..	..	..	..
	1995	..	..	..	..	..	..	..	..	..	..
	1990	..	..	..	..	..	..	..	..	..	..
Syrian Arab Republic الجمهورية العربية السورية											
	2007	..	..	..	..	..	..	..	..	..	..
	2006	30.6	26.8	..	..	..	..	..	..	..	..
	2005	30.4	26.6	..	..	..	..	..	..	..	..
	2004	30.1	26.3	..	..	..	..	..	..	..	..
	2003	..	..	..	..	..	..	..	..	..	..
	2002	..	..	..	..	..	..	..	..	..	..
	2001	..	..	..	..	..	..	..	..	..	..
	2000	28.9	25.1	..	..	..	..	..	..	..	..
	1995	..	..	..	..	..	..	..	..	..	..
	1990	..	..	..	..	..	..	..	..	..	..

* Preliminary data.

* بيانات أولية.

TABLE 24. CRUDE MARRIAGE AND DIVORCE RATES SINCE 1990*

الجدول ٢٤ - معدلات الزواج والطلاق الخام منذ عام ١٩٩٠(*)

| | | Marriages الزواج | | | | | | Divorces الطلاق | | | | | |
Country البلد	Year السنة	Nationals مواطنين	Non-nationals غير مواطنين	Urban حضر	Rural ريف	Total number of marriages مجموع حالات الزواج	Crude marriage rates (per thousand) معدل الزواج الخام (في الألف)	Nationals مواطنين	Non-nationals غير مواطنين	Urban حضر	Rural ريف	Total number of divorces مجموع حالات الطلاق	Crude divorce rates (per thousand population) معدل الطلاق الخام (في الألف)
Bahrain البحرين	2006	...	...	...	...	4 724	6.4	...	...	...	...	1 141	1.5
	2005	...	...	...	...	4 669	6.4	...	...	...	...	1 051	1.5
	2004	...	...	...	...	4 929	6.9	...	...	...	...	1 030	1.5
	2003	...	...	...	...	5 373	7.7	...	...	...	...	923	1.3
	2002	...	...	...	...	4 909	7.2	...	...	...	...	838	1.2
	2001	...	...	...	...	4 504	6.8	...	...	...	...	801	1.2
	2000	...	...	...	...	3 963	6.1	...	...	...	...	769	1.2
	1995	...	...	...	...	3 321	5.7	...	...	...	...	691	1.2
	1990	...	...	...	...	2 942	6.0	...	...	...	...	590	1.2
Egypt مصر	2007a	...	...	204 910	409 938	614 848	8.1	...	...	35 283	42 595	77 878	1.0
	2006	...	...	168 323	354 564	522 887	7.1	...	...	31 858	33 603	65 461	0.9
	2005	...	...	170 556	352 195	522 751	7.2	...	...	32 256	32 791	65 047	0.9
	2004	...	...	175 361	375 348	550 709	7.7	...	...	33 136	31 360	64 496	0.9
	2003	...	...	185 880	351 212	537 092	7.6	...	...	34 425	35 442	69 867	1.0
	2002	...	...	183 538	326 979	510 517	7.4	...	...	33 971	36 098	70 069	1.0
	2001	...	...	167 616	289 918	457 534	6.8	...	...	35 192	35 087	70 279	1.0
	2000	...	...	213 079	379 302	592 381	8.9	...	...	32 305	36 686	68 991	1.0
	1995	...	...	...	...	470 513	7.8	...	...	...	...	67 653	1.1
	1990	...	...	...	...	405 141	7.3	...	...	...	...	67 195	1.2
Iraq العراق	2007	...	...	...	...	...	...	...	...	...	...	...	...
	2006	...	...	...	...	...	...	...	...	...	...	...	...

TABLE 24 (continued)
الجدول ٢٤ (تابع)

Country البلد	Year السنة	Marriages الزواج						Divorces الطلاق					
		Nationals مواطنين	Non-nationals غير مواطنين	Urban حضر	Rural ريف	Total number of marriages مجموع حالات الزواج	Crude marriage rates (per thousand) معدل الزواج الخام (في الألف)	Nationals مواطنين	Non-nationals غير مواطنين	Urban حضر	Rural ريف	Total number of divorces مجموع حالات الطلاق	Crude divorce rates (per thousand population) معدل الطلاق الخام (في الألف)
	2005	...	...	...	...	262 554	9.6	...	...	...	...	...	...
	2004	...	...	...	...	256 494	9.5	...	...	...	...	...	...
	2003	...	...	...	...	...	...	...	...	...	...	...	...
	2002	...	...	...	...	...	...	...	...	...	...	...	...
	2001	...	...	...	...	171 134	6.8	...	...	...	...	...	...
	2000	...	...	...	...	120 692	5.6	...	...	...	...	33 161	1.5
	1995	...	...	...	...	143 518	7.8	...	...	...	...	...	...
	1990	...	...	...	...	...	...	...	...	...	...	...	...
Jordan الأردن	2007	...	...	...	...	60 548	10.2	...	...	...	...	11 793	2.0
	2006	...	...	...	...	59 335	10.4	...	...	...	...	11 413	2.0
	2005	...	...	...	...	56 418	10.2	...	...	...	...	10 231	1.8
	2004	...	...	...	...	53 754	10.0	...	...	...	...	9 791	1.8
	2003	...	...	...	...	48 784	9.4	...	...	...	...	9 022	1.7
	2002	...	...	...	...	46 873	9.3	...	...	...	...	9 032	1.8
	2001	...	...	...	...	49 794	10.1	...	...	...	...	9 017	1.8
	2000	...	...	...	...	45 618	9.5	...	...	...	...	8 241	1.7
	1995	...	...	...	...	35 501	8.2	...	...	...	...	6 315	1.5
	1990	...	...	...	...	32 706	10.1	...	...	...	...	5 074	1.6
Kuwait الكويت	2007	10 851	2 464	...	...	13 315	4.7	3 818	1 127	...	...	4 945	1.7
	2006	9 776	2 808	...	...	12 584	4.5	3 201	1 038	...	...	4 239	1.5
	2005	9 296	3 123	...	...	12 419	4.6	3 400	1 138	...	...	4 538	1.7
	2004	9 291	3 068	...	...	12 359	4.7	3 654	1 245	...	...	4 899	1.9

TABLE 24 (continued)
الجدول ٢٤ (تابع)

Country البلد	Year السنة	Marriages الزواج						Divorces الطلاق					
		Nationals مواطنون	Non-nationals غير مواطنين	Urban حضر	Rural ريف	Total number of marriages مجموع حالات الزواج	Crude marriage rates (per thousand) معدل الزواج الخام (في الألف)	Nationals مواطنون	Non-nationals غير مواطنين	Urban حضر	Rural ريف	Total number of divorces مجموع حالات الطلاق	Crude divorce rates (per thousand population) معدل الطلاق الخام (في الألف)
البلد	2003	9 355	2 891	…	…	12 246	4.8	3 041	957	…	…	3 998	1.6
	2002	9 231	2 742	…	…	11 973	4.9	2 968	923	…	…	3 891	1.6
	2001	8 677	3 153	…	…	11 830	5.1	2 885	966	…	…	3 851	1.6
	2000	7 847	2 938	…	…	10 785	4.8	2 737	912	…	…	3 649	1.6
	1995	…	…	…	…	9 515	5.5	…	…	…	…	3 015	1.7
	1990	…	…	…	…	…	…	…	…	…	…	…	…
Lebanon لبنان	2007	…	…	…	…	35 796	8.7	…	…	…	…	6 342	1.5
	2006	…	…	…	…	29 078	7.2	…	…	…	…	4 388	1.1
	2005	…	…	…	…	29 705	7.4	…	…	…	…	4 746	1.2
	2004	…	…	…	…	30 014	7.6	…	…	…	…	4 372	1.1
	2003	…	…	…	…	30 636	7.8	…	…	…	…	4 328	1.1
	2002	…	…	…	…	31 653	8.2	…	…	…	…	4 060	1.0
	2001	…	…	…	…	32 225	8.4	…	…	…	…	4 480	1.2
	2000	…	…	…	…	32 564	8.6	…	…	…	…	4 282	1.1
	1995	…	…	…	…	30 758	8.8	…	…	…	…	3 869	1.1
	1990	…	…	…	…	29 945	10.1	…	…	…	…	3 026	1.0
Oman عُمان	2007	…	…	…	…	…	…	…	…	…	…	…	…
	2006	…	…	…	…	…	…	…	…	…	…	…	…
	2005	…	…	…	…	…	…	…	…	…	…	…	…
	2004	…	…	…	…	…	…	…	…	…	…	…	…
	2003	487 486	376 715	160 244 a/	327 781 a/	864 201	351.4	22 950	3 409	…	…	26 359	10.7
	2002	…	…	…	…	…	…	…	…	…	…	…	…

-68-

TABLE 24 (continued)
الجدول ٢٤ (تابع)

Country	Year السنة	Marriages الزواج — Nationals مواطنون	Non-nationals غير مواطنين	Urban حضر	Rural ريف	Total number of marriages مجموع حالات الزواج	Crude marriage rates (per thousand population) معدل الزواج الخام (في الألف)	Divorces الطلاق — Nationals مواطنون	Non-nationals غير مواطنين	Urban حضر	Rural ريف	Total number of divorces مجموع حالات الطلاق	Crude divorce rates (per thousand population) معدل الطلاق الخام (في الألف)
	2001	...	...	...	...	...	...	...	...	...	...	...	...
	2000	...	...	...	...	...	...	...	...	...	...	...	...
Palestine فلسطين	2007	65 370	...	...	...	...	16.3	8 086	...	...	...	...	2.0
	2006	56 466	...	...	...	...	14.5	7 512	...	...	...	...	1.9
	2005	57 752	...	...	...	...	15.4	8 422	...	...	...	...	2.2
	2004	55 268	...	...	...	...	15.2	7 922	...	...	...	...	2.2
	2003	52 534	...	...	...	...	15.0	7 318	...	...	...	...	2.2
	2002	46 222	...	...	...	...	13.6	6 092	...	...	...	...	1.8
	2001	49 270	...	...	...	...	15.1	7 374	...	...	...	...	2.3
	2000	47 780	...	...	...	...	15.2	7 092	...	...	...	...	2.3
	1996	41 472	...	...	...	...	15.3	6 988	...	...	...	...	2.6
Qatar قطر	2007	2 013	1193	...	...	3 206	3.8	721	276	...	...	997	1.2
	2006	2 023	996	...	...	3 019	3.7	604	222	...	...	826	1.0
	2005	1 848	886	...	...	2 734	3.4	469	174	...	...	643	0.8
	2004	1 730	919	...	...	2 649	3.5	564	223	...	...	787	1.0
	2003	1 773	777	...	...	2 550	3.5	581	209	...	...	790	1.1
	2002	1 593	758	...	...	2 351	3.4	552	180	...	...	732	1.1
	2001	1 549	645	...	...	2 194	3.4	448	118	...	...	566	0.9
	2000	1 483	613	...	...	2 096	3.4	471	144	...	...	615	1.0
	1995	...	...	...	...	1 488	2.8	...	...	...	...	474	0.9
	1990	...	...	...	...	1 370	2.9	...	...	...	...	359	0.8

TABLE 24 (continued)

الجدول ٢٤ (تابع)

| Country البلد | Year السنة | Marriages الزواج | | | | | Divorces الطلاق | | | | |
		Nationals مواطنين	Non-nationals غير مواطنين	Urban حضر	Rural ريف	Total number of marriages مجموع حالات الزواج	Crude marriage rates (per thousand) معدل الزواج الخام (في الألف)	Nationals مواطنين	Non-nationals غير مواطنين	Urban حضر	Rural ريف	Total number of divorces مجموع حالات الطلاق	Crude divorce rates (per thousand population) معدل الطلاق الخام (في الألف)
Saudi Arabia المملكة العربية السعودية													
	2006	...	...	...	...	119 294	4.9	...	...	...	...	24 862	1.0
	2005	...	...	...	...	105 066	4.4	...	...	...	...	24 318	1.0
	2004	...	...	...	...	111 063	4.8	...	...	...	...	24 435	1.1
	2003	...	...	...	...	98 343	4.4	...	...	...	...	20 794	0.9
	2002	...	...	...	...	90 982	4.2	...	...	...	...	18 765	0.9
	2001	...	...	...	...	81 576	3.8	...	...	...	...	16 725	0.8
	2000	...	...	...	...	79 595	3.8	...	...	...	...	18 583	0.9
	1993	...	...	...	...	67 934	3.9	...	...	...	...	13 227	0.8
Syrian Arab Republic[b] الجمهورية العربية السورية[b]													
	2007	237 592	...	...	...	...	11.9	19 506	...	...	...	...	1.0
	2006	205 557	...	...	...	...	10.6	19 984	...	...	...	...	1.0
	2005	179 075	...	...	...	...	9.5	17 821	...	...	...	...	0.9
	2004	178 166	...	...	...	...	9.7	17 336	...	...	...	...	0.9
	2003	204 944	...	...	...	...	11.5	14 314	...	...	...	...	0.8
	2002	174 449	...	...	...	...	10.0	14 314	...	...	...	...	0.8
	2001	153 842	...	...	...	...	9.1	13 077	...	...	...	...	0.8
	2000	139 843	...	...	...	...	8.5	11 863	...	...	...	...	0.7
	1995	120 146	...	...	...	...	8.2	10 540	...	...	...	...	0.7
	1990	91 705	...	...	...	...	7.2	8 342	...	...	...	...	0.7

TABLE 24 (continued)
الجدول ٢٤ (تابع)

Country	Year	Marriages						Divorces					
		Nationals	Non-nationals	Urban	Rural	Total number of marriages	Crude marriage rates (per thousand population)	Nationals	Non-nationals	Urban	Rural	Total number of divorces	Crude divorce rates (per thousand population)
United Arab Emirates الإمارات العربية المتحدة													
	2007	...	...	...	...	...	...	...	...	...	...	...	...
	2006	...	...	...	...	...	...	...	...	...	...	...	...
	2005	...	...	...	...	12 751	3.1	...	...	...	...	3 364	0.8
	2004	...	...	...	...	12 794	3.2	...	...	...	...	3 577	0.9
	2003	...	...	...	...	12 277	3.2	...	...	...	...	3 243	0.9
	2002	...	...	...	...	11 285	3.1	...	...	...	...	3 390	0.9
	2001	...	...	...	...	10 030	2.9	...	...	...	...	2 832	0.8
	2000	...	...	...	...	8 970	2.8	...	...	...	...	2 392	0.7
	1995	...	...	...	...	6 475	2.7	...	...	...	...	2 256	0.9
	1990	...	...	...	...	7 357	3.9	...	...	...	...	1 994	1.1
Yemen اليمن													
	2004	...	...	...	...	715	0.0	...	...	...	...	33	0.0
	2003	...	...	...	...	600	0.0	...	...	...	...	104	0.0
	2002	...	...	...	...	10 934	0.6	...	...	...	...	998	0.1
	2001	...	...	...	...	9 120	0.5	...	...	...	...	617	0.0
	2000	...	...	...	...	5 375	0.3	...	...	...	...	507	0.0
	1997	...	...	...	...	11 448	0.7	...	...	...	...	2 249	0.1

* Rates are calculated on the basis of population data from *World Population Prospects: The 2006 Revision*.

a/ Preliminary data.

b/ Data refer to Syrian nationals only. Population estimates from national sources.

* احتسبت المعدلات استناداً إلى بيانات السكان الواردة في منشور الأمم المتحدة التوقعات السكانية في العالم: تنقيح عام ٢٠٠٦".

(أ) بيانات أولية.

(ب) تشمل البيانات المواطنين السوريين فقط. تقدير ات السكان من مصادر وطنية.

TECHNICAL NOTES

1. Crude birth rate (CBR)

The number of live births (B^t_o) occurring during a particular calendar year (or average annual births in a given period) in a particular area per 1,000 mid-year total population (P):

$$CBR = \frac{B^t_o}{P} \times 1000$$

2. Crude death rate (CDR)

The number of deaths in a particular area during a calendar year (or annual average deaths in a given period) (D^t_o) per 1,000 of mid-year total population (P):

$$CDR = \frac{D^t_o}{P} \times 1000$$

3. Rate of natural increase (r)

The difference between the number of live births and deaths occurring in a year, expressed as a percentage of the base population of that year. This measure of population change excludes the effects of migration expressed as a percentage of the base population of that year:

$$RNI = \frac{B^t_o - D^t_o}{P} \times 100$$

$$\text{or } RNI = \frac{CBR - CDR}{10}$$

١- معدل المواليد الخام

وهو عدد المواليد الأحياء (B^t_o) خلال سنة معينة (أو المتوسط السنوي للولادات في فترة معينة) لكل ألف من مجموع السكان في منتصف السنة (P). ويحسب كالتالي:

٢- معدل الوفيات الخام

وهو عدد الوفيات التي تحدث في مكان معين خلال سنة معينة (أو المتوسط السنوي للوفيات في فترة معينة) (D^t_o) لكل ألف من مجموع السكان في منتصف السنة (P). ويحسب كالتالي:

٣- معدل الزيادة الطبيعية

وهو الفرق بين عدد المواليد الأحياء وعدد الوفيات التي تحصل في غضون سنة، محسوب كنسبة مئوية من القاعدة السكانية. وهذا القياس تغير القاعدة السكانية يستثني تأثيرات الهجرة المحسوبة كنسبة مئوية من القاعدة السكانية في تلك السنة. ويحسب كالتالي:

4. Foetal death rate (FDR)

The number of foetal deaths occurring in the population of a given geographical area in a given year per 1,000 total births (live births plus foetal deaths):

وهو عدد وفيات الأجنة التي تحدث بين سكان منطقة جغرافية معينة في سنة معينة لكل ألف من مجموع المواليد (ولادات المواليد الأحياء والأجنة المتوفاة) ويحسب كالتالي:

$$FDR = \frac{\text{foetal deaths}}{\text{live births} + \text{foetal deaths}} \times 1000$$

5. Infant mortality rate (IMR)

The number of infant deaths (excluding foetal deaths) between birth and first birthday in the population of a given area during a calendar year (or annual average infant death rate in a given period) (D^t_o) per 1,000 live births (B^t):

وهو عدد وفيات الرضع (الذي لا يشمل وفيات الأجنة) التي تحدث في سكان منطقة معينة خلال سنة معينة (أو المتوسط السنوي لوفيات الرضع في فترة معينة) (D^t_o) لكل ألف من المواليد الأحياء (B^t) ويحسب كالتالي:

$$IMR = \frac{D^t_o}{B^t} \times 1000$$

6. Child mortality rate (U5MR)

The probability of dying before the age of five, expressed as deaths under the age of five per 1,000 live births:

وهو أرجحية الوفاة قبل بلوغ سن الخامسة، ويقاس بعدد وفيات الأطفال تحت سن الخامسة لكل ألف من المواليد الأحياء، ويحسب كالتالي:

$$U5MR = \frac{\text{child deaths}}{\text{live births}} \times 1000$$

7. Maternal mortality ratio (MMR)

The number of deaths from puerperal causes in the female population of a given geographical area in a given year per 100,000 live births in that area in that year:

وهي عدد الوفيات الناتجة عن أسباب نفاسية بين سكان منطقة جغرافية معينة في سنة معينة لكل مائة ألف من المواليد الأحياء في تلك المنطقة وذلك في تلك السنة. ويحسب كالتالي:

$$MMR = \frac{\text{maternal deaths}}{\text{live births}} \times 100,000$$

-73-

8. General fertility rate (GFR)

The number of live births in a particular calendar year (or average live births in a given period) in a given area (B'_0) per 1,000 mid-year female population of childbearing age (15-49) (F_{15-49}):

$$GFR = \frac{B'_0}{F_{15-49}} \times 1000$$

9. Age-specific fertility rate (ASFR)

The number of births ($_nB_x$) per 1,000 women in a particular age group ($_nF_x$) during a calendar year:

$$ASFR = \frac{_nB_x}{_nF_x} \times 1000$$

10. Total fertility rate (TFR)

The number of children that would be born to a woman if she were to live to the end of her childbearing years (15-49) and if the likelihood of her giving birth to children at any given age were to be the currently-prevailing age-specific fertility rate. It is the total of all the age-specific fertility rates defined over a five-year interval (n):

$$TFR = n \sum_{15}^{49} \left(\frac{_nB_x}{_nF_x} \right)$$

٨- معدل الخصوبة العام

وهو عدد المواليد الأحياء في سنة معينة (أو متوسط عدد المواليد الأحياء في فترة معينة) لكل ألف امرأة في سن الإنجاب (من عمر ١٥ إلى ٤٩ سنة) (F_{15-49}) من مجموع عدد المواليد في فترة معينة (B'_0) (لكل ألف من مجموع السكان في منتصف السنة. ويحسب كالتالي:

$$GFR = \frac{B'_0}{F_{15-49}} \times 1000$$

٩- معدل الخصوبة العمرية

وهو عدد المواليد ($_nB_x$) لكل ألف امرأة من فئة عمرية معينة ($_nF_x$) خلال سنة معينة. ويحسب كالتالي:

$$ASFR = \frac{_nB_x}{_nF_x} \times 1000$$

١٠- معدل الخصوبة الكلي

وهو عدد الأطفال الذين من المفترض أن يولدوا لامرأة معينة إذا عاشت حتى نهاية فترتها الإنجابية (من عمر ١٥ إلى ٤٩ سنة) وإذا كانت احتمالات أن تلد أطفالاً في أي عمر معين تتم وفقاً لمعدل الخصوبة العمرية السائد خلال السنة المعينة. وبذلك يجمع كل معدلات الخصوبة الكلية بجمع احتساب معدل الخصوبة العمرية المحددة في فترات فاصلة من خمس سنوات (n)، وذلك وفق المعادلة التالية:

$$TFR = n \sum_{15}^{49} \left(\frac{_nB_x}{_nF_x} \right)$$

11. Gross reproduction rate (GRR)

The GRR is based on ASFR and identical to TFR, but refers only to female births. It indicates how many daughters a woman would bear during her lifetime if, throughout her reproductive life, she were subject to the age-specific rate of bearing female children as recorded for a particular year or another given interval. A close approximation of GRR can be obtained by multiplying TFR by the proportion of female births to all births in a given period.

12. Mean age at childbearing

The mean age of women when their children are born. For a given calendar year, the mean age of women at childbearing is the weighted average of the different ages (the reproductive period is generally considered to be 15-49 years of age), using as weights the age-specific fertility rates (ASFR) (that is, the number of live births to mothers of age x to the average female population of age x). Depending on the country, the age is either the age reached during the year or the age at last birthday.

13. Crude death rate by cause (CDRc)

The number of deaths from a given cause or group of causes in a given area during a calendar year (or annual average across a given period) (D_c^t) per 100,000 of the mid-year total population (P):

$$CDRc = \frac{D_c^t}{P} \times 100,000$$

11 – معدل الإحلال الإجمالي

وهو مبني على أساس معدل الخصوبة العمرية (ASFR) ويناظر تماماً معدل الخصوبة الكلية (TFR)، غير أنه يعود إلى المواليد الإناث فقط. ويشير إلى عدد المواليد لامرأة ما خلال فترتها الإنجابية، إذا انطبق عليها معدل الخصوبة العمرية لإحلال الإناث المسجل خلال سنة معينة أو فترة زمنية فاصلة معينة. ويمكن الحصول على تقدير قريب جداً لمعدل الإحلال الإجمالي (GRR) بضرب معدل الخصوبة الكلية في نسبة المواليد الإناث من إجمالي المواليد في فترة معينة.

12 – متوسط عمر المرأة عند الإنجاب

يُعتبر متوسط عمر المرأة عند الإنجاب في سنة معينة المتوسط المرجح للأعمار المختلفة (حيث تُعتبر الفترة الإنجابية عموماً بين سن 15 و49 سنة)، ويُحتسب باستخدام معدلات الخصوبة العمرية كعامل مرجّح (أي عدد المواليد الأحياء لمجموع الأمهات بسن (x) إلى متوسط عدد النساء بسن (x) من السكان؛ وتكون السن إما السن التي تم بلوغها خلال السنة المعينة أو السن في آخر عيد ميلاد).

13 – معدل الوفيات الخام بحسب السبب

وهو عدد الوفيات الناتجة عن سبب معين أو مجموعة معينة من الأسباب في منطقة معينة خلال سنة معينة (أو المتوسط السنوي لفترة زمنية معينة) (D_c^t) لكل مائة ألف من السكان في منتصف السنة (P). ويُحسب كالتالي:

١٤ – متوسط العمر عند الزواج الأول

وهو متوسط العمر لأي فرد عند الزواج الأول. ويمكن احتساب متوسط العمر عند الزواج الأول بحسب السن باستخدام معدلات الزواج الأول بحسب السن (أي عدد الزيجات في سنة معينة (x) نسبة الى متوسط عدد السكان في السن (x) وباستخدام هذه الطريقة يكون متوسط العمر غير مرجّح، أي لا يُؤخذ بعين الاعتبار عدد النساء أو الرجال في كل سن.

٥١ – معدل الزواج الخام

وهو نسبة عدد الزيجات في منطقة معينة خلال سنة معينة (أو المتوسط السنوي خلال فترة معينة) (M^t_0) الى متوسط عدد السكان (P) في المنطقة نفسها والفترة نفسها لكل ألف من السكان. ويحسب كالتالي:

$$CMR = \frac{M^t_0}{P} \times 1000$$

١٦ – معدل الطلاق الخام

وهو نسبة عدد حالات الطلاق في منطقة معينة خلال سنة معينة (أو المتوسط السنوي خلال فترة معينة) (Div^t_0) الى متوسط عدد السكان (P) في المنطقة نفسها والفترة نفسها لكل ألف من السكان. ويحسب كالتالي:

$$Cdiv = \frac{Div^t_0}{P} \times 1000$$

---

14. Mean age at first marriage

The mean age at which an individual first marries. For a given calendar year, it can be calculated using the first marriage rates by age (that is, the number of first marriages at age x in relation to the average population of age x). Using this calculation, the mean age is not weighted, meaning that the number of women or men at each age is not taken into account.

15. Crude marriage rate (CMR)

The ratio of the number of marriages in a given area during a calendar year (or annual average across a given period) (M^t_0) to the average population (P) in the same period and the same area per 1,000 inhabitants:

$$CMR = \frac{M^t_0}{P} \times 1000$$

16. Crude divorce rate (Cdiv)

The ratio of the number of divorces in a given area during a calendar year (or annual average across a given period) (Div^t_0) to the average population (P) in the same period and the same area per 1,000 inhabitants:

$$Cdiv = \frac{Div^t_0}{P} \times 1000$$

مسرد المصطلحات الإحصائية العربية

معدل الخصوبة العمرية	عدد المواليد لنساء من فئة عمرية معينة مقسوما على عدد النساء من تلك الفئة. والفئات العمرية المستخدمة هي: ١٩-١٥ سنة، و٢٤-٢٠ سنة، و٢٩-٢٥ سنة، و٣٤-٣٠ سنة، و٣٩-٣٥ سنة، و٤٤-٤٠ سنة، و٤٩-٤٥ سنة. وتشير البيانات إلى فترات من خمس سنوات تبدأ في ١ تموز/يوليو من سنة البداية وتنتهي في ٣٠ حزيران/يونيو من سنة النهاية.
القاعدة السكانية	عدد السكان في منطقة معينة (مثل بلد، أو مقاطعة أو مدينة) ينطبق عليها معدل حيوي معين، أي أنه القاسم في معدل الولادات أو الوفيات، حيث يحدد عدد السكان من بيانات التعداد.
الولادات	المتوسط السنوي لعدد الولادات خلال فترة معينة. وتشير البيانات التي ترد بالآلاف، إلى فترات من خمس سنوات تبدأ في ١ تموز/يوليو من سنة البداية وتنتهي في ٣٠ حزيران/يونيو من سنة النهاية.
الولادات بحسب الفئة العمرية للأم	عدد الولادات خلال فترة معينة مصنفة بحسب الفئة العمرية للأم (١٩-١٥) سنة، و٢٤-٢٠ سنة، و٢٩-٢٥ سنة، و٣٤-٣٠ سنة، و٣٩-٣٥ سنة، و٤٤-٤٠ سنة، و٤٩-٤٥ سنة). وتشير البيانات، التي ترد بالآلاف، إلى فترات من خمس سنوات تبدأ في ١ تموز/يوليو من سنة البداية وتنتهي في ٣٠ حزيران/يونيو من سنة النهاية.
التعداد	مسح يُجرى حول مجموعة كاملة من المواصفات المشمولة بالمراقبة والتي تميز مجموعة سكان معينين أو عالما معينا.

GLOSSARY OF STATISTICAL TERMS

Age-specific fertility rate
Number of births to women in a particular age group, divided by the number of women in that age group. The age groups used are 15-19, 20-24, 25-29, 30-34, 35-39, 40-44 and 45-49. The data refer to five-year periods running from 1 July of the initial year to 30 June of the final year.

Base population
The number of people in a given area (for example, a nation, province or city) to which a specific vital rate applies; that is, the denominator of the crude birth rate or death rate, the population being determined from census data.

Births
Average annual number of births over a given period. The data refer to five-year periods running from 1 July of the initial year to 30 June of the final year and data are presented in thousands.

Births by age group of mother
Number of births over a given period classified by age group of mother (15-19, 20-24, 25-29, 30-34, 35-39, 40-44 and 45-49). The data refer to five-year periods running from 1 July of the initial year to 30 June of the final year. Data are presented in thousands.

Census
A survey conducted on the full set of observation objects belonging to a given population or universe.

English term	English description	المصطلح	الوصف
Census population	Latest census population, covering all residents, regardless of legal status or citizenship, except for refugees not permanently settled in the country of asylum. Data are presented by nationals and non nationals, by sex, and by rural and urban areas per country. In addition, census population data for each of the above disaggregations are presented by five-year age group for each country.	تعداد السكان	آخر تعداد للسكان يشمل كل المقيمين، بصرف النظر عن وضعهم القانوني أو جنسيتهم، باستثناء اللاجئين غير المقيمين بشكل دائم في بلد اللجوء. وترد البيانات بحسب المواطنين وغير المواطنين، وبحسب النوع الاجتماعي، والمناطق الريفية والحضرية لكل بلد. وبالإضافة إلى ذلك، ترد البيانات حول كل من هذه الجوانب وفق فئات عمرية من خمس سنوات لكل بلد.
Crude birth rate	Number of births over a given year per 1,000 population.	معدل المواليد الخام	عدد المواليد في سنة معينة لكل ألف من السكان.
Crude death rate	Number of deaths over a given year per 1,000 population.	معدل الوفيات الخام	عدد الوفيات في سنة معينة لكل ألف من السكان.
Crude marriage rate	The number of marriages occurring in the population of a given geographical area during a given year per 1,000 mid-year total population of the given area during the same year.	معدل الزواج الخام	عدد الزيجات التي تحدث بين سكان منطقة جغرافية معينة خلال سنة معينة لكل ألف من السكان في منتصف السنة لتلك المنطقة وخلال تلك السنة.
Deaths by sex	Number of deaths over a given period, classified by sex (male, female and both sexes combined). The data refer to five-year periods running from 1 July of the initial year to 30 June of the final year and data are presented in thousands.	الوفيات بحسب الجنس	عدد الوفيات خلال فترة معينة مصنفة بحسب النوع الاجتماعي (أي الذكور والإناث والفئتان معاً). وتشير البيانات التي ترد بالألاف، إلى فترات من خمس سنوات تبدأ في ١ تموز/يوليو من سنة البداية وتنتهي في ٣٠ حزيران/يونيو من سنة النهاية.
Deaths under age 1	Number of deaths under age 1 over a given period. The data refer to five-year periods running from 1 July of the initial year to 30 June of the final year and data are presented in thousands.	الوفيات دون السنة من العمر	عدد الوفيات التي تحدث قبل بلوغ السنة الأولى من العمر خلال فترة معينة. وتشير البيانات التي ترد بالألاف، إلى فترات من خمس سنوات تبدأ في ١ تموز/يوليو من سنة البداية وتنتهي في ٣٠ حزيران/يونيو من سنة النهاية.

الوفيات دون العمر سنوات من العمر	الخمس	عدد الوفيات التي تحدث قبل بلوغ السنة الخامسة من العمر خلال فترة معينة. وتشير البيانات، التي ترد بالآلاف، إلى فترات من خمس سنوات تبدأ في ١ تموز/يوليو من سنة البداية وتنتهي في ٣٠ حزيران/يونيو من سنة النهاية.
نسب الإعالة		نسبة الإعالة الكلية هي نسبة مجموع عدد السكان بعمر صفر إلى ١٤ سنة وعدد السكان بعمر ٦٥ سنة وما فوق إلى عدد السكان بعمر ١٥ إلى ٦٤ سنة. ونسبة إعالة الأطفال هي نسبة عدد السكان بعمر صفر إلى ١٤ سنة إلى عدد السكان بعمر ١٥ إلى ٦٤ سنة. ونسبة إعالة المسنين هي نسبة عدد السكان بعمر ٦٥ سنة وما فوق إلى عدد السكان بعمر ١٥ إلى ٦٤ سنة. وترد كل النسب كعدد المعالين لكل مائة شخص بعمر العمل أو من ١٥ إلى ٦٤ سنة.
الطلاق		الفسخ النهائي للزواج، أي انفصال الزوج والزوجة على نحو يعطي الطرفين حق الزواج من جديد بموجب أحكام مدنية أو دينية و/أو أحكام أخرى وفقاً لقوانين كل بلد.
التقدير		عملية استنتاج قيمة رقمية لقيم سكانية مجهولة من خلال بيانات غير مكتملة، مثل النموذج.
معدلات الزواج بحسب العمر	الأول	عدد الزيجات الأولى للنساء (أو الرجال) في سن (x) نسبة إلى متوسط عدد الإناث (أو الذكور) من السكان في سن (x). وتكون السن، بحسب البلد المعني، إما السن التي تم بلوغها في آخر عيد ميلاد.

Deaths under age 5

Number of deaths under age 5 over a given period. The data refer to five-year periods running from 1 July of the initial year to 30 June of the final year. Data are presented in thousands.

Dependency ratios

The total dependency ratio is the ratio of the sum of the population aged 0-14 plus that aged 65 and over to the population aged 15-64. The child dependency ratio is the ratio of the population aged 0-14 to the population aged 15-64. The old-age dependency ratio is the ratio of the population aged 65 years and over to the population aged 15-64. All ratios are presented as number of dependants per 100 persons of working age (15-64).

Divorce

The final dissolution of a marriage, that is, the separation of husband and wife which confers on the parties the right to remarriage under civil, religious and/or other provisions, according to the laws of each country.

Estimation

The process of inferring the numerical value of unknown population values from incomplete data, such as a sample.

First marriage rates by age

The number of first marriages of women (or men) of age x in relation to the average female (or male) population of age x. Depending on the country, the age is either the age reached during the year or the age at last birthday.

Infant mortality	The probability (expressed as deaths per 1,000 live births) of a child born in a specified year dying before reaching the age of 1 if subject to current age-specific mortality rates.	وفيات الرضع	بحسب المعدلات السابقة للوفيات، أرجحية وفاة طفل مولود في سنة معينة قبل بلوغه السنة الأولى من عمره، وتُقاس بعدد الوفيات لكل ألف من المواليد الأحياء.
Life expectancy by sex	The average number of years of life expected by a hypothetical cohort of individuals if subject throughout their lives to the mortality rates of a given period, expressed in years.	العمر المتوقع بحسب الجنس	متوسط عدد السنوات التي من المتوقع أن يعيشها فوج من السكان إذا انطبقت عليه المعدلات السائدة في فترة معينة، وتُقاس بالسنوات.
Marriage	The act, ceremony or process by which the legal relationship of husband and wife is constituted. The legality of the union may be established by civil, religious or other means, as recognized by the laws of each country.	الزواج	العمل أو الاحتفال أو الإجراء الذي ينشأ بموجبه الرباط الشرعي بين الزوج والزوجة. وينشأ هذا الرباط بطرق مدنية أو دينية أو غيرها، تبعاً للقوانين المعمول بها في كل بلد.
Mean age at first marriage	The weighted average of the age at first marriage, using as weights the age-specific marriage rates for first marriages only.	متوسط العمر عند الزواج الأول	المتوسط المرجّح للعمر عند الزواج الأول، ويُحسب باستخدام معدلات الزواج العمرية للزيجات الأولى فقط كعوامل مرجحة.
Mortality under age 5	Probability of death between birth and fifth birthday, expressed as deaths per 1,000 births.	الوفاة قبل سن الخامسة	أرجحية حدوث الوفاة في وقت بين الولادة والسنة الخامسة من العمر، وتُحسب بعدد الوفيات لكل ألف من المواليد.
Net reproduction rate	The average number of daughters a hypothetical cohort of women would have at the end of their reproductive period if they were subject throughout their lives to the fertility rates and mortality rates of a given period, expressed as number of daughters per woman.	معدل الإحلال الصافي	متوسط عدد المواليد الإناث لفوج افتراضي من النساء في نهاية فترتين الإنجابية ومعدلات الوفاة إذا انطبقت عليهن طول حياتهن معدلات الخصوبة ومعدلات الوفاة لفترة معينة، ويُحسب كعدد الإناث لكل امرأة.
Percentage urban	Urban population as a percentage of the total population.	النسبة المئوية الحضرية	سكان المناطق الحضرية كنسبة مئوية من مجموع السكان.

Term	Definition	المصطلح	التعريف
Percentage rural	Rural population as a percentage of the total population.	النسبة المئوية الريفية	سكان المناطق الريفية كنسبة مئوية من مجموع السكان.
Place of occurrence	The civil subdivision of a country (district, county, municipality, province, department or state) in which a live birth or death, foetal death, marriage or divorce takes place.	مكان الحدوث	جزء من التقسيم المدني لبلد معين، أي المقاطعة أو الإقليم أو البلدية أو الإدارة أو الولاية حيث تحدث الولادة الحية أو الوفاة أو وفاة الجنين أو الزواج أو الطلاق.
Population sex ratio	Number of males per 100 females in the population.	نسبة الجنس من السكان	عدد الذكور لكل مائة أنثى من السكان.
Population	De facto population of a country, area or region as at 1 July of the year indicated. Figures are presented in thousands.	السكان	العدد الفعلي لسكان بلد أو منطقة ما في 1 تموز/يوليو من السنة المعنية. وترد البيانات بالآلاف.
Population by age group	De facto population as at 1 July of the year indicated (presented in thousands), and the percentage of the total population that it represents. The population age groups are: 0-4, 0-14, 5-14, 6-11, 12-14, 15-17, 18-23, 15-24, 15-59, 15-64, 60 or over, 65 or over and 80 or over.	السكان بحسب الفئة العمرية	العدد الفعلي للسكان في 1 تموز/يوليو من السنة المعنية للفئة العمرية المعنية (وترد البيانات بالآلاف) والنسبة التي يمثلها هذ العدد من مجموع السكان. والفئات العمرية للسكان هي التالية: صفر-4، صفر-14، 5-14، 6-11، 12-14، 15-17، 18-23، 15-24، 15-59، 15-64، 60 وما فوق، 65 وما فوق و80 وما فوق.
Population at risk	The population that is exposed to the occurrence of a vital event, for example, the total population in the case of deaths or the legally-married population in the case of divorces.	السكان المعرّضون	السكان المعرّضون لحدوث واقعة حيوية، وعلى سبيل المثال، مجموع السكان إذا كان الأمر يتعلق بالوفيات أو السكان المتزوجون قانونياً إذا كان الأمر يتعلق بحالات الطلاق.
Population by five-year age group and sex	De facto population as at 1 July of the year indicated, classified by sex (male, female and both sexes combined) and by five-year age groups (0-4, 5-9, 10-14 [...] 95-99, 100+). Data are presented in thousands.	السكان بحسب فئات عمرية من خمس سنوات والجنس	العدد الفعلي للسكان في 1 تموز/يوليو من السنة المعنية، مصنفين بحسب النوع الاجتماعي (أي الذكور والإناث، والفئتين معاً) وبحسب فئات عمرية من خمس سنوات (صفر-4 سنوات، 5 إلى 9 سنوات، 10 إلى 14 سنة [...] 95 إلى 99 سنة، 100 سنة وما فوق). وترد البيانات بالآلاف.

Population census	عملية جمع وتجهيز وتقييم وتحليل ونشر أو توزيع البيانات المتعلقة بالخصائص الديمغرافية والاقتصادية والاجتماعية لجميع الأفراد بلد معين أو جزء محدد جيداً من البلد وفي زمن معين.	تعداد السكان
The process of collecting, compiling, evaluating, analyzing and publishing or otherwise disseminating demographic, economic and social data pertaining, at a specified time, to all persons in a country or in a well-delimited part of a country.		
Population estimates	التقديرات السكانية للبلدان، مصنفة بحسب النوع الاجتماعي، ومقدمة وفقا لسلاسل زمنية من عام ٢٠٠٠ إلى عام ٢٠٠٧.	التقديرات السكانية
Country estimates, disaggregated by sex, presented in a time series from 2000 until 2007.		
Population projections	التقديرات بشأن ما سيكون عليه الحجم الإجمالي للسكان أو تركيبهم في المستقبل.	التوقعات السكانية
Estimates of total size or composition of populations in the future.		
Proportion	نوع خاص من النسبة حيث يكون القاسم كمية تمثل مجمل الفئة المعنية المشمولة بالبحث، وحيث يكون البسط هو جزء منها.	النسبة
A special type of ratio in which the denominator is a quantity that represents the whole of a given group under investigation and the numerator is a subset of it.		
Rate	حدوث وقائع ما خلال فترة فاصلة محددة. وهو أيضا قياس تردد ظاهرة اهتمام معينة.	المعدل
The occurrence of events over a specific interval. Also refers to the measure of the frequency of a phenomenon of interest.		
Rate of natural increase	معدل المواليد الخام ناقصا معدل الوفيات الخام. وهو يمثل جزءا من النمو السكاني تحدده الولادات والوفيات فقط.	معدل الزيادة الطبيعية
Crude birth rate minus crude death rate. Represents the portion of population growth (or decline) determined exclusively by births and deaths.		
Ratio	العلاقة بين كميتين تقاسان بالوحدة القياسية ذاتها، محسوبة بنسبة إحدى الكميتين على الأخرى. وليس للنتيجة وحدة قياس.	النسبة
The relationship between two quantities measured in the same unit, expressed as one value divided by another. The result has no unit.		

تسجيل الوقائع الحيوية		التسجيل المتواصل والدائم والقسري لحدوث الوقائع الحيوية، وبعض الخصائص المحددة أو الوصفية المتصلة بها في كل بلد، وتتضمن هذه الوقائع الوفيات الأجنة والزيجات وروفيات الأجنة والزيجات والطلاق والانفصال القضائي، وإلغاء الزواج، والتبني، والاعتراف القانوني ببنوة الأطفال الطبيعيين والاعتراف القانوني ببنوة الأطفال غير الشرعيين.
سكان الريف		العدد الفعلي للسكان المقيمين في مناطق مصنفة ريفية (وهو الفرق بين مجموع سكان البلد وعدد سكان المناطق الحضرية). وتشير البيانات إلى ١ تموز/يوليو من السنة المبينة وترد بالألوف.
نسبة الجنسين عند الولادة		عدد المواليد الذكور لكل أنثى مولودة.
معدل الخصوبة الكلي		متوسط عدد الأطفال الذين تلدهم مجموعة افتراضية من النساء في نهاية فترتهن الإنجابية إذا انطبقت عليهن طول حياتهن معدلات الخصوبة السائدة في فترة معينة ولم يتعرضن للموت. ويرد هذا المعدل كعدد الأطفال لكل امرأة.

Registration of vital events	Continuous, permanent and compulsory recording of the occurrence of vital events, together with certain identifying or descriptive characteristics relating to such events, regulated by the civil code, laws or regulations of each country. Such vital events may include live births, deaths, foetal deaths, marriages, divorces, judicial separations, marriage annulments, adoptions, recognitions (legal acknowledgement of natural children) and legitimations.
Rural population	De facto population living in areas classified as rural (that is, the difference between the total population of a country and its urban population). Data refer to 1 July of the year indicated and are presented in thousands.
Sex ratio at birth	Number of male births per single female birth.
Total fertility rate	The average number of children a hypothetical cohort of women would have at the end of their reproductive period if they were subject throughout their lives to the fertility rates of a given period and not subject to mortality; expressed as number of children per woman.

Total first marriage rate
معدل الزيجات الأولى (مجموع)

The mean number of first marriages in a given year, calculated by adding the first marriage rates by age of women (or men) for the year in question. For the purposes of calculation, the number of women (or men) at each age is assumed to be the same. It does not separate out the different generations and is not the first marriage rate of any specific generation; rather, it is the first marriage rate of a hypothetical generation subjected at each age to the current marriage conditions.

متوسط عدد الزيجات الأولى في سنة معينة ويحسب بإضافة معدلات الزواج الأول بحسب عمر المرأة (أو الرجل) للسنة المعنية. ولأغراض الحساب، يفترض أن عدد النساء (أو الرجال) هو نفسه في كل عمر. وهذا المعدل لا يفصل بين الأجيال وليس معدل الزواج الأول لأي جيل هو معدل الزواج الأول لجيل مفترض تنطبق عليه في كل مرحلة عمرية شروط الزواج السائدة.

Urban population
سكان الحضر

Given national differences in the characteristics that distinguish urban from rural areas, the distinction between urban and rural population is not amenable to a single definition applicable to all countries. National definitions are commonly based on size of locality; any population that is not urban is considered rural.

في ضوء اختلافات المميزة بين البلدان تتعلق بالخصائص المميزة بين المناطق الحضرية وسكان الريف على تعريف واحد ينطبق على جميع البلدان. وتستند التعريفات الوطنية عادة إلى حجم الموقع، كما أن سكان أي مناطق غير المناطق الحضرية يعتبرون من سكان الريف.

Vital event
الواقعة الحيوية

A live birth, death, foetal death, marriage, divorce, adoption, legitimation, recognition of parenthood, annulment of marriage or legal separation.

الولادة الحية، والوفاة وموت الجنين، والزواج، والطلاق، والتبني، والاعتراف القانوني بالأبوة، وإلغاء الزواج أو الانفصال القانوني.

Women aged 15-49
النساء بعمر ١٥ إلى ٤٩ سنة

Number of women aged 15-49 as at 1 July of the year indicated (presented in thousands) and that number as a percentage of the total female population as at 1 July of that year.

عدد النساء بعمر ١٥ إلى ٤٩ سنة في ١ تموز/يوليو من السنة المعينة ويحسب بالألوف، وكنسبة من مجموع الإناث من السكان في ١ تموز/يوليو من تلك السنة.